"This book wil̲l̲ ̲h̲e̲l̲p̲ ̲y̲o̲u̲ ̲s̲e̲e̲ ̲b̲e̲y̲o̲r̲
a dating partner will help you forn
—f̲.

"You want the best for your little cubs. You also want to share your life with someone. Can you do both? You can trust Ron Deal to shoot straight with you about kids, dating, and finding lasting love. Find the answers you need in this book."

—Dr. Kevin Leman
New York Times bestselling author of *Have a New Kid by Friday*

"Entering the dating arena as a single parent is scary. Don't do it alone. In *Dating and the Single Parent*, Ron Deal points out the common pitfalls and gives wise counsel in how to navigate the waters. I highly recommend it."

—Gary Chapman, PhD
Bestselling author, *The Five Love Languages*

"Your choice is to get real or to get blindsided. In the crackling electricity of a dating relationship, it's easy for single parents to overlook huge issues that cause deep personal pain as well as permanent damage to their children. Ron Deal shows you how to avoid the big mistakes and build successful, lasting relationships. *Dating and the Single Parent* is a must-read for all solo parents."

—Steve Grissom
Founder, DivorceCare and Single & Parenting

"I wish I'd had a resource like *Dating and the Single Parent* during my twelve years of single parenthood. Great stuff! Ron Deal helps you avoid common pitfalls and gives you a usable road map to experiencing healthy relationship in the future. He also offers great counsel on guarding the hearts of your kids. If you only read one single-parenting book this year, make it this one!"

—Elsa Kok Colopy, author, speaker, and former editor of the
Single-Parent Family edition of *Focus on the Family* magazine

"Once again Ron Deal has written a powerful book, a much-needed resource, to help those who may be considering remarriage one day. Ron's authentic and frank narrative and advice are a must-read for single parents. From the beginning, Ron points out that 'coupleness does not equal familyness,' and this and many other of his valuable insights can help ensure you have healthy and successful relationships."

—Paula Bisacre,
Publisher, www.RemarriageWorks.com

Books by Ron L. Deal

FROM BETHANY HOUSE PUBLISHERS

Dating and the Single Parent

The Smart Stepfamily Marriage (with David H. Olson)

The Smart Stepdad

The Smart Stepfamily

The Smart Stepfamily Small Group Resource DVD

and Participant's Guide

The Smart Stepmom (with Laura Petherbridge)

FROM FAMILYLIFE PUBLISHING

Life in a Blender (booklet for kids)

The Smart Stepfamily Marriage Small-Group Study Guide

Dating
and the
Single
Parent

RON L. DEAL

BETHANY HOUSE PUBLISHERS
a division of Baker Publishing Group
Minneapolis, Minnesota

002000440524

© 2012 by Ron L. Deal

Published by Bethany House Publishers
11400 Hampshire Avenue South
Bloomington, Minnesota 55438
www.bethanyhouse.com

Bethany House Publishers is a division of
Baker Publishing Group, Grand Rapids, Michigan

Printed in the United States of America

Library of Congress Cataloging-in-Publication Data
Deal, Ron L.
    Dating and the single parent : are you ready to date?, talking with your kids, avoiding a big mistake, finding lasting love / Ron L. Deal ; foreword by Dennis Rainey.
        p.   cm.
    Includes bibliographical references.
    Summary: "Remarriage and stepfamily expert guides single parents through the labyrinth of decisions and emotional ups and downs of dating with kids so they can make the best decision possible. From a Christian perspective"— Provided by publisher.
    ISBN 978-0-7642-0697-9 (pbk. : alk. paper)
    1. Single parents—Social life and customs. 2. Dating (Social customs)— Religious aspects—Christianity. 3. Children of single parents—Psychology. 4. Parent and child—Religious aspects—Christianity. 5. Remarriage—Religious aspects—Christianity. I. Title.
HQ759.915.D43 2012
306.85′6—dc23   2012028748

The Internet addresses, email addresses, and phone numbers in this book are accurate at the time of publication. They are provided as a resource. Baker Publishing Group does not endorse them or vouch for their content or permanence.

In keeping with biblical principles of creation stewardship, Baker Publishing Group advocates the responsible use of our natural resources. As a member of the Green Press Initiative, our company uses recycled paper when possible. The text paper of this book is composed in part of post-consumer waste.

Cover design by Eric Walljasper
Author is represented by MacGregor Literary, Inc.

15 16 17 18 19 20 21   9 8 7 6 5 4 3

To single parents and your children

May God's grace, strength, and wisdom be with you as you navigate the many decision points ahead.

ACKNOWLEDGMENTS

Through the years I've learned so much from the single parents I've counseled and worked beside in ministry. Thank you for your courageous vulnerability and willingness to share your lives, dreams, and struggles. I'm humbled by what you accomplish every single day on behalf of your kids. I'm especially grateful to the single parents who served in a focus group for this book. The time you took to respond to questions, read the manuscript, and share your insights will bless thousands of single parents and their children. I am truly grateful.

A special word of thanks to Bethany House for your continued support of my writing; five books together—what a ride! Ellen (my editor), you have always brought clarity to my writing, but this time I owe you a special thank-you for nurturing the book and my ideas as I wrote. You really shaped this project more than you realize and made it much more than it would have been without you. I'm indebted.

My agent, Chip MacGregor, is the best. Two parts coach, one part counselor, three parts strategist, and best-part friend.

And finally, I want to show appreciation once again to my wife, Nan. Thanks for believing in me.

CONTENTS

FOREWORD

Like many single people, you probably long to share your life with someone. Perhaps your heart jumps and you get all tingly when a prospect comes along. But what of your parental heart? As a single parent or the dating partner of a single parent you intuitively know that dating is different because someone else is involved—the kids. Dating isn't just about the two of you, making dating and a potential marriage more complicated than ever. And because kids are involved and the stakes are higher this time around, I'm confident you want to make wise dating decisions.

As a parent, you may wonder how dating will affect your children. Are they ready? Are you ready? If you're dating someone with kids, you wonder what to expect and how to tell if you can make a blended family work. This book will answer those questions and more.

Forty-two percent of adults in the U.S. have a step relationship. At FamilyLife's Weekend to Remember marriage getaways, we've found that up to 30 percent of couples who attend are in blended families. But sadly, two-thirds of marriages where one or both partners bring children into the relationship end in divorce. In view of this need, FamilyLife has been delighted to welcome Ron Deal to our ministry. A licensed marriage and family therapist who has over two decades of experience working with blended families, Ron will reveal why relationships with kids in the mix are so much more complex. And he'll show you what you can do as you begin a relationship to navigate those difficulties and prepare for a successful marriage.

Ron shares that "coupleness" and "familyness" are not the same thing. As good as a dating relationship might feel, it's nothing without familyness, and ultimately familyness is what creates a legacy. This book will help you see beyond the tingly feelings to determine if a dating partner will help you form a healthy family.

If you're a single parent, Ron's going to ask you practical questions to see if you're emotionally and relationally ready to date. He will share with you conversations you need to have with your kids before you date and once the dating has started, and he will help you decide when and how to introduce kids to the person you may be more than just casually interested in.

If you're dating someone with kids, Ron will prepare you for the unique family dynamics that might otherwise blindside you after the honeymoon's over. He'll explain why you can't expect that marrying someone with kids will instantly give you the family you may have always wanted.

Ron will also discuss the yellow and red lights to watch out for in the relationship, and reveal the traps of online dating.

He has some hard truths to tell parents. For example, even though the person you're dating may feel like your life partner, your children may not be ready to share you with them. He will also encourage you to consider whether dating is beneficial for you and the kids right now, and tell you why and when it might be better to wait.

For over thirty-six years my wife, Barbara, and I have been working with families, equipping people with the skills they need for marriage. We know storms are inevitable. It's critical to determine whether the person you're dating is someone who's going to lay a firm foundation with you to withstand them. Ron can help you anticipate rough weather particular to blended families and give you wisdom on knowing if your dating partner will help you survive the turbulent storms that you *will* encounter. Ron will equip you with what you need to establish a solid foundation and build your house on The Rock of Jesus Christ (Matthew 7:24–27).

Proverbs says, "Let the wise listen and add to their learning, and let the discerning get guidance" (1:5). In this book you'll find invaluable spiritual guidance from one of America's leading blended family experts. Listen to Ron's advice and become wise.

Dr. Dennis Rainey
President, FamilyLife
April 2012

PREFACE

> **PROMISE:**
> This book will tell you the hard truth about single-parent dating. Side effects may include greater discernment about the path to marriage, finding lasting love, creating family unity, and avoiding big mistakes for you and the kids. Please be advised: not all fantasies will become reality.

Get-rich-quick books promise a fast track to wealth beyond your dreams with little risk, little effort, and no time required. Dating books often promise the same. *Find lasting love in three easy steps—no risk required!* I refuse to do that to you. I respect you and care about your kids too much to tell you everything you want to hear and offer simplistic advice.

If you want to get rich, you need to apply wise investment practices and self-discipline over an extended period of time. If you want to date well with children in the picture and make a solid decision about getting married, you need to gain wisdom about the dating process, know the risks and challenges for both you and your children, and make careful decisions—over an extended period of time.

This book promises to tell you the truth about single-parent dating. In fact, some of you will find hard truths you don't want to hear—and you'll be irritated with me for saying them. Please know these hard truths are intended for your benefit and the well-being of your children. If family unity is the wealth you ultimately desire, read the entire book and be willing to receive the hard truths. Relational wealth will come about as a result.

For twenty years I have been working with stepfamilies as a therapist, conference speaker, and ministry leader. The most common comment I hear from married couples in blended families is, "We had no idea what we were getting into."

After reading this book, that *won't* be you.

INTRODUCTION
STRIVING FOR LOVE

The Daily, an online and Apple iPad news service, reported that on March 19, 2011, Forrest Lunsway, age one hundred, and Rose Pollard, age ninety, qualified for a Guinness World Record as the oldest couple ever to marry. Rose's advice to dating couples: "Take your time and get to know one another. Get to know if you like all the things that person stands for. If they have the same values." I guess she meant that, because the couple dated for thirty years (no rush to marriage here!) and then married on Forrest's one-hundredth birthday at their local senior center in Orange County, California.[1]

People the world over—no matter their age—believe in romantic love. For example, while more and more Americans say that marriage is becoming obsolete for society, a fewer number think marriage is obsolete for them.[2] Most people still want to get married. We believe in marriage, strive for it, long for it, and actively pursue it.[3]

We are created in the image of a loving God with the deepest desire to, like him, love and be loved. This includes, in general, having loving relationships with extended family and friends, and specifically includes the desire to mate with another in an exclusive pair-bond. God himself pointed out that the first thing in creation that wasn't good was that man was alone. Keep in mind that man wasn't completely "alone"; he had complete access to and oneness with God. But apparently that wasn't sufficient, given man's design. Adam needed something else. We, male and female, were made with the need to connect and be partnered with a member of the other gender.

Adam's same existential ache to be partnered with someone is felt by the unmarried today. It's what opens us to romance and pulls us toward the idea of a pair-bond relationship. And it's what gives us what I jokingly call marital amnesia, that is, the willingness to date again even after a painful divorce (LOL). People in the midst of a horrible divorce who vow "never again to be vulnerable to rejection" often find themselves a few years or even months later falling for another person. The possibility of love leads us to temporarily forget what it's like to be in pain, and forever invites us to look with optimism toward a future with love. The sense of aloneness *pulls* us toward love. But if the ache of loneliness pulls, the ache of pain *pushes.*

The pit of loss, whether stemming from a divorce, the death of a spouse, or the rejection of a boyfriend/girlfriend with whom you share a child, is dark and easily overwhelming—and no one wants to stay there long. In the pit, depression, sadness, guilt, devastation, rejection, and a sense of being lost abound. Needless to say, these are unwelcome infections, and if you are not careful, your medication of choice will be romance. Notice I didn't say "love," I said "romance." Romance and infatuation have an intoxicating effect that gives the appearance of fixing pain, and boy is it attractive. If there is one clear vulnerability in life, it is anything or any feeling that promises to lift you out of the pit of pain. This may be drugs or alcohol, pornography, religiosity, excessive work, anything that provides a rush of adrenaline, or a new relationship. The cocaine of attention seems to work wonders when all you know is the pit. But buyer beware: This drug has a short shelf life and can ultimately cause more destruction!

At some level, whether for God-given *pull* reasons or medicinal *push* ones, most single people are striving for love and shared romance with another person. Maybe you are just beginning to entertain the idea of dating and are hoping this book can help you navigate the terrain. Or maybe you have dated a few times, maybe even fell in love again, but found the experience confusing.[4] (One person said, "It's weird trying to figure out how to enter the dating world, and pretty depressing, to be honest. I feel like an awkward teenager all over again.") Or perhaps you believe you've already found the love of your life and you're wondering about your kids. In any case, this book will help.

> ### If You Are Dating a Single Parent
>
> When reading sections of this book written specifically to single parents be sure to assess whether the person you are dating is giving proper consideration to the concepts. If not, invite them to read the book along with you. If they continue to ignore the wisdom shared, don't assume your goodwill can make up for their short-sightedness.

Single-parent dating includes complicated questions:

- So far my kids and I have survived our loss—how will the transition to my dating complicate our survival?
- How do I know I'm ready or that my kids are ready for me to start dating?
- What if the person I date brings harm to my kids? How would I know if they are a sexual predator?
- How is dating or marriage going to affect my kids and my parenting?
- How do I introduce someone to my kids—and what if they don't like each other?
- How will marriage and blended family living impact my kids—and how can I guarantee that I or they won't be hurt again?

The person dating a single parent has questions, too:

- How do I date in a crowd (i.e., with kids in the picture)?
- How do I make a good first impression on the kids? What do I do if they don't like me or give me dirty looks?
- If I fall in love with their parent, what would my role be as a stepparent? Could I handle it?
- What's the ex-factor? How do I deal with their ex, and how much of a negative influence will they be?

These and many other questions will be addressed in this book. Considered together, these questions illuminate a crucial insight for both single parents and those dating them that we will return to again and again: When kids are involved, dating is not just about finding a mate but beginning a family.

THE CATCH: COMPETING ATTACHMENTS

In adoptive and biological families, couples come together before children enter the picture. When coupleness precedes familyness, as I like to say, the marriage serves as the source and foundation of the family unit. Here's why that's important: When marriage forms the foundation of the family, every other relationship in the family is an outgrowth of the marriage and systemically supports it and lives in harmony with it. When children are born to a couple, the resulting parent-child relationships don't intrinsically compete with the couple's marriage. They may vie for time and energy, but their very presence doesn't inherently compete with the marriage itself. Parent-child relationships naturally draw strength and security from the marriage and in turn feed and support the marriage. When the marriage precedes children, family attachments mutually strengthen and feed one another.

However, when a single parent moves toward a love relationship with someone who is not the child's parent, a competing attachment is formed. To the child, the parent's love and increasing dedication to a new partner do not naturally strengthen the child's relationship with the parent, but compete with it. Likewise, stepparents often feel left out and perhaps jealous when their spouse spends time with their stepkids. Because familyness pre-dated coupleness, relationships compete.

Here's another way to articulate the contrast. In first families, everyone is rooting for the couple's success, especially the kids. When Mom and Dad are happy, life is as it should be. When parents are at odds with each other, kids in biological families hope they'll resolve their issues and live at peace. But in blended families, children aren't as invested in the success of the couple as the couple is, and on occasion they are dead set against it. Relationships in biological families naturally synergize and support each other; new relationships in blended families naturally compete with the emotional attachments that preceded the new marriage.

That's why I always cringe when I hear a single parent say one reason they want to find a new partner is so their children will have a father or a mother. While it's true that a stepfather, for example, can eventually fill some of the masculine gaps in a child's life, a mother's hope that a stepfather will fill the "daddy-hole" in a child's heart is misguided. She needs to understand that bringing a man into her children's

---

Your Wisdom Shared on Facebook/ SmartStepfamilies

What do you wish you had known before getting remarried?

"I was prepared. I had read the books and intellectually understood the process. But living as a blended family is infinitely tougher than I thought it would be."—Lara S.

"I wish that I hadn't tried to replace my kids' dad with my husband. I thought that since their dad was literally an absentee father, their stepdad could become their 'real' dad with all the rights and privileges that come with being a biological father."—Marilyn E.

"Wish I would have known how hard it was going to be and could have prepared my heart for this hurt better."—Teresa S.

"I wish I would have known how hurtful stepkids can be and the damage they do on a guilt-ridden father. Read, get counseling, attend a great church, and take the online Couple Checkup BEFORE the 'I Do's'!"—Sophia H.

lives very well may destabilize (at least for a time) her children's world, not bring stability to it. At a minimum, it will decentralize them from receiving her full attention—a significant change for children who have already experienced great loss—and may make them feel in competition with their stepfather.

Recognizing this truth will better inform your striving for love. Embracing this truth as a single parent will lessen your expectations of instantly becoming a happy family, lower your stress about finding someone who will fill the parental gaps in your child's life, and hopefully help you to relax about finding a mate. Embracing this truth as someone dating a single parent will help you not feel rejected if the kids are slow to warm up to you; it's still difficult, but at least you know this response is common and not necessarily a personal rejection of you. Not recognizing this truth sets you up—whether you are the single parent or dating partner—to send me an email of confusion and frustration.

MY RECURRING EMAIL

Have you ever had a recurring nightmare? I get a recurring email. You can fill in the specifics, but the basic structure is the same. Melissa's email is a good example:

> *Kevin and I have been married almost two years. . . . We did not have any premarital preparation. . . . We decided to marry a few months after we met. I have three sons ages . . . and Kevin has two kids ages . . . I thought this would be easy because we felt right for each other—boy was I wrong. Absolutely dead wrong! We have struggled for two years. . . . We are so in love with each other, but we can't come to terms on matters of parenting and stepparenting, and the boys are jealous of my relationship with Kevin. I wish we would have waited a little longer to marry. Can you help us?*
>
> *—Melissa*

Now, here's what you need to know: Kevin and Melissa are good people. In fact, they are godly, upstanding, going-to-heaven people. They just didn't know what they didn't know. And they let the push of ache (trying to run from the pit of pain) and pull of love (the desire for attachment) dictate their dating and decisions about marriage instead of letting wisdom do that for them. In short, they fell prey to their own blinders. (Regrettably, I have to pause and share this irony of ironies—just now as I was writing this section, I actually got another version of this recurring email! Except this time it ended with "I just got served divorce papers." Married just fourteen months and their blended family is over. My heart breaks for them. It doesn't have to end this way for you.)

WISDOM AND FOLLY

The first nine chapters of Proverbs in the Bible present a contrast between those who embrace the wisdom of God and those who reject it for foolishness. The two sides of this contrast are personalized as Wisdom and Folly, who call out to and try to entice passersby. The contrast is profound. Wisdom provides understanding and the knowledge of God; Folly provides simplemindedness and a lack of judgment. Wisdom provides victory, a shield of protection, and peace to the soul; Folly leaves one exposed to evil and filled with anxiety. Wisdom offers discretion to walk straight paths of blessing and rescues one from lustful and adulterous enticements; Folly leaves one to walk in dark ways and fall prey to the influence of lust. Wisdom extends life and brings prosperity as one wins the favor of both men and God; Folly offers a short and difficult, undisciplined life.

I beg you to heed the call of Wisdom regarding your relationships, your family decisions, and your parenting or you might as well start drafting your email to me now. Folly offers no discernment; it is only interested in pursuing the passions of the moment and the quick fixes of infatuation and fantasy. Folly will crumble at the feet of blended family challenges because it refuses to take a hard look at reality; it will only bring about difficult paths for your life. Wisdom, on the other hand, considers life and love through the lens of eternity and bases decisions about dating and marriage not solely on coupleness alone, but on familyness, as well.

I implore you: Dedicate yourself to reading this entire book, taking its wisdom to heart. Because it is uncommon, Wisdom usually challenges. Likewise, this book will challenge your thinking, your emotions, your walk with the Lord, your parenting, and your pursuit of love. Take it to heart, discuss it with friends, and consider its insights. I certainly don't know how this Wisdom will impact your life or future decisions; that is for you and God to work out. But I do believe, whatever it brings, it will be for the best.

REMARRIAGE ADVOCATE?

On one occasion while conducting a media interview, a host introduced me as an advocate for remarriage. After the interview when we had time to talk, I clarified what Wisdom has taught me about blended families. I'm not an advocate for remarriage, I shared. I am most definitely an advocate for first families because that is God's design, and what he designs is always for our best. When biological families split, I continued, I advocate for reconciliation. Forgiveness and reconciliation are very close to the heart of God, and when possible, reconciling and creating a God-honoring marriage always serves the couple and children's best interests (I do recognize that reconciling and creating a mutually loving and serving relationship is not always possible). When couples find themselves in a blended family, I am an advocate for helping them to honor their marriage covenant and become a model of God's love and healing grace.

But to be honest, I told the host, I really don't know what to advocate for when it comes to single parents. On one hand, remarriage and blended family living can be a positive, redemptive force in the lives of children and adults. I've seen that happen time and time again and always celebrate God gracing the lives of children and parents through their stepfamily. But that's not always the case. To be candid, some blended families are a disaster—especially when the adults haven't done their homework on how to combine a family—and just expose children to more heartache.

The point I'm making is that from the standpoint of a child's well-being, raising children in a single-parent home is a good option and can be just as redemptive as a healthy blended family. So when it comes to single parents, I advocate first for empowered single parents who are equipped to go the distance with their kids if necessary, and then for smart dating and careful discernment about marriage when love comes along.

Balancing your desire for love with the kids' need for stability and emotional safety is tough. You'll need as much wisdom and maturity as you can get to walk this line well. My hope is that this book will be a trusted friend along the way.

I promise to be honest with you in this book. Online matchmaking services will not be honest with you. They want to sell you on a convenient love. I want to sell you on a wisdom that will guide and protect each step of your family journey (and, ironically, will make the odds of you finding a satisfying love more likely). I believe this wisdom will serve you well as you make decisions about singleness, dating, and stepfamily marriage. Your decisions about such matters will have emotional, psychological, and spiritual impact for generations to come and should not be taken lightly. Invite God into the journey, make him Lord of your personal needs and your parenting, and let him lead. Every decision brings challenges. But if the Lord is in the decision, the challenges can be overcome.

Discussion Questions

1. What societal trends and attitudes about marriage are you aware of? How have those influenced your friends' or your opinions about dating and marriage?

2. Rate your sense of "aloneness" on a scale of 1 to 10. In what ways is it pulling you toward dating and/or marriage?

3. Rate any ache of pain in your life (1 to 10). How does it push you toward dating and/or marriage? Be sure to write down the major hurts that make up your pit of pain and loss.

4. If you are dating a single parent, what concerns do you have about your relationship with the children? Your potential role as a stepparent? Before reading this chapter, how much had you thought about the impact of "familyness" on "coupleness"?

5. As it relates to your dating, what concerns for your children haunt you the most?

6. This chapter states, "Relationships in biological families naturally synergize and support each other; new relationships in blended families naturally compete with the emotional attachments that preceded the new marriage." In what way is this a new idea for you? How does it impact your thinking about dating? How does it inform your fantasies of building an instantly harmonious family?

7. What Wisdom have you seen in how other people date, and what Folly have you witnessed?

8. React and discuss this statement: "From the standpoint of a child's well-being, raising children in a single-parent home is a good option and can be just as redemptive as a healthy blended family."

Getting Past Butterflies and Warm Fuzzies

Have you ever noticed how easy it is to romanticize the process of dating? First you meet someone and sparks fly, fireworks blaze the sky, and unexplainable chemistry draws you together. Butterflies fill your stomach and warm fuzzies your heart—and before you know it, you're in love.

Okay, let's get past that right now, shall we?

Initial chemistry may be what draws you together, but you better add some substance quick. The introduction suggested that because coupleness does not equal familyness, couples should avoid getting so enthralled with a dating partner that they fail to keep in mind the complexity of becoming a family. I encourage you to keep this essential concept in the forefront of your mind at all times, even while taking initial steps to meet someone. To that end, the next few chapters will help you explore your emotional, psychological, spiritual, and relational readiness for dating and at the same time will keep an eye on the kids and the impact dating has on them. Let's begin by getting a sense of the purpose and overall process of dating for both you and the kids.

Chapter 1

Dating in a Crowd: Dating With Purpose

Our whole family is dating this guy.
Rachel, 22 years old

Sometimes kids say it best. When asked what she wishes her mom would do differently while dating, Rachel—a smart young graduate student—replied, "I wish she would recognize her own impulsivity and emotional roller coaster. She does and says things without recognizing that to some extent our whole family is dating this guy. This year I came home four times from college and he was in town every single time. After I went back to campus each time, Mom said, 'I never get to see you!' Yes, well, that's because you were with your boy. I just wish they would hurry up and get married so they would be a bit less interesting to one another."

Dating in a crowd is tough. The kids are engaged, at least on some level, even when you don't think they are. Choosing to be with one party generally means the other party is left waiting. And everyone has strong emotions and opinions about who is involved and what the outcome is—in other words, the whole family is dating. *Table for twenty!*

For the two people directly involved, dating is hard enough; add the kids, ex-spouses, extended family, and friends, and you better have a plan and purpose in your dating or you'll likely waste a lot of time and wander from romance to romance with a lot of heartbreak along the way. The most consistent mistakes I see in people who have repeated failed dating (and later, marriage) relationships are these: they don't have a purpose in dating; they lack an intentional process to their dating; they don't have an appreciation for the complexity of dating in a crowd; they don't take their children's needs and feelings into consideration enough; and they don't realize that the growing connections between children and future stepparents or stepsiblings established during dating may shift toward distance and conflict after the wedding (it's this last truth that really catches people by surprise—I'll say more about this later).

As we begin our journey together, I'd like to recommend a purpose for your dating and present an overall process to dating that will help you know when you're on target for a good start. Many of the specifics of this process will be discussed in more depth throughout the remainder of the book, but I do want you to get a sense of what to expect, from pre-dating preparation, to making a decision for marriage, to anticipating the hot/cold responses of children.

PURPOSE IN DATING

Does your dating have purpose? *What do you mean, Ron? Isn't the purpose of dating to find the right person—my soul mate?* No, it isn't. Let me explain.

I always question when I hear someone say they are looking for their soul mate, because for most people, finding someone has nothing to do with their soul or eternity. A 2001 study of dating attitudes of twenty-year-olds found that an overwhelming majority (94 percent) of never-married singles agree that "when you marry, you want your spouse to be your soul mate, first and foremost." But only 42 percent believe "it is important to find a spouse who shares your religion."[1] Are you kidding me? How can they remotely qualify as a soul mate and not share your core beliefs and guiding spiritual convictions? (I guess to them, a soul mate has little to do with spirituality.) Remember, single parents, this person is going to have an eternal influence on your kids. Isn't finding someone with your same spiritual beliefs of the utmost importance?

No, apparently what the average person looking for a soul mate is really saying is, "I'm looking for the person who is easy for me to love; someone who will fulfill my needs and who knows just how to love me." Sounds pretty selfish, doesn't it? Soul-mate shopping is nothing more than consumerism applied to dating. The mentality is to date as many people as you can—or as one writer said it, test drive people to see which you like best—and stop when you find the one that meets your expectations and needs.[2]

The problem with this attitude is fourfold. First, it assumes the test driver contributes nothing to the quality of the developing relationship, which, of course, you do. Second, the consumer's criteria for their purchase is completely selfish. Even if you find someone who seems to make you happy, they won't be able to sustain it forever. This usually isn't obvious until marriage, which is when most people begin to think, *Maybe you weren't my soul mate after all—I must have made a mistake.* Third, it mistakenly places too much emphasis on your happiness as a couple and not enough on the role the stepparent will have as a parent. And fourth, the consumer attitude toward dating assumes that God has purposed marriage to make us happy. He has, but not in the way most expect.

A Match Made in Heaven: God's Purpose in Relationships, Marriage, and Family

Our God loves us beyond anything we can imagine, and he will go to great lengths to pursue us and foster a deep relationship with us. He will even go to a cross to rescue us from the slavery of our sin. But God doesn't stop his pursuit of us after our initial rescue. Through discipling us to be more like Jesus, he deepens our walk with him. I believe that family life is God's best tool for discipling us. From the cradle to the grave, he is growing us up in maturity, faith, and knowledge—and he is using relationships to train us.

When we're children, God uses our family to teach us important lessons about obedience, submission, and respect for authority. Learning these lessons makes it more likely that we'll gain respect for God's authority. In parenting, God teaches us about nurture, providing for those you love, and how far you will go to rescue one of your own. We also learn about free will (he lets us create life and struggle with the reality of not being able to control it!) and humility (praying for your kids will drive you to your knees!). In friendships, God teaches us about loyalty and living in community. In being single, God teaches us about trusting him with our aloneness and not turning marriage into an idol. God uses marriage to teach us about commitment, sacrifice, forgiveness, and selfless love. In the physical, emotional, and spiritual depth of sex, God teaches us about surrender, vulnerability, and oneness. In crisis, God reminds us of kingdom priorities and the limits of materialism, and he recalibrates our faith and trust toward him. And in facing death, God invites us to live in light of what is eternal. In all of these life experiences and relationships, God invites us to walk with him: "to act justly and to love mercy and to walk humbly with your God" (Micah 6:8).

In all of this, God is purposing to make us holy and healthy and eternally happy. He knows what is best for us, and each relationship and season of family life invites us to trust him and know him more deeply. And therein lies the rub. Making us eternally happy usually doesn't satisfy our selfishness today; instead, it requires us to grow up a lot emotionally—which is painful. Ask yourself if you are open to what God is teaching you about him in your singleness. Are you pursuing him as much as he is pursuing you? Is your singleness helping you to see him more clearly and trust him more deeply, or are you instead telling him what he should be doing for you? Are you open to maturing in this season of life, or do you assume that you need marriage to be fulfilled?

Knowing Yourself

Take time to reflect on the questions in this section. Knowing what motivates you in dating is very important.

And what about dating? When you meet someone, is whether they make you happy or holy the standard by which you choose to engage them? Do you lose sight of the Lord when you fix your sights on a man or woman, or can you keep your eye on your eternal love while exploring an earthly love? In what way is your purpose in dating blocking God's purpose for you in dating?

With God's goals in mind, I suggest that the purpose of dating for single parents is threefold:

- to discern if together you and this other person can walk humbly with God with a common heart, faith, value system, and approach to life;
- to discern if you can love the person sacrificially without reservation,[3] and trust that they will do the same for you;
- to discern if the children involved in your union would be graced by your common commitment to the Lord and combined families.

If your purposes for dating don't pass this smell test, slow down or stop altogether. You may be naturally attracted to someone and enjoy time together, but if after a brief dating period you are just wandering aimlessly, it's probably time to stop playing around. If dating reveals at any point that your life trajectories (faith walk, parenting, family situations, values, etc.) are divergent, back away. This is not a game. Is it okay to date on occasion purely for recreational purposes? Yes, as long as you don't let children get emotionally wrapped up in the dating partner (more about this in a later chapter) and the other person is aware of your intentions and the limits of the relationship. But dating is not a goal in and of itself. Instead, think of dating as the process you go through to become married. That helps to keep the ultimate purpose in mind.

THE PROCESS OF DATING

Having a spiritually determined purpose in dating will help to set your attitude in the right direction. It also helps to have a sense of the process or stages of dating. Thinking through the overall process helps you to know where you are in the journey and what tasks lie ahead. It also helps you gauge the depth of a developing relationship and whether it will hold water.

In general, single parent dating will move through the following stages: It starts, if you are the single parent, by preparing yourself and the kids for dating; if you are single without children, it starts by assessing your openness to dating someone with kids and welcoming them into your life. From there, the stages consist of forming an initial couple relationship; initial dating partner and child relationships; serious dating and deepening couple and dating partner-child bonds; making decisions about marriage; and preparing for a wedding and blended family living.

Dating Process FAQs

From a stage perspective, the dating process is straightforward and clear. But questions about managing the process abound. The following are some frequently asked questions with answers that give perspective to the journey.

> ## When the Kid Is an Adult
>
> Empty-nest couples are often very surprised to learn that later-life blended families with adult stepchildren have just as many adjustment issues as do families with children still at home. The specific issues vary, but don't naïvely assume everyone will be open to a new love in your life.

But before diving into the FAQs, let me speak about a perspective to avoid. Society has created many unspoken benchmarks for dating couples. They are meant to help individuals gauge the dating process, but most of them are ambiguous, simplistic, and shallow. Don't let these questions guide your thinking about your dating relationship: *Is this person good-looking and do I get points just for standing beside them? Are they wealthy or do they at least have the potential to become wealthy? Do they hang out with the right people? Are they sexually experienced (because I don't want to be with a novice)? Have we had sex yet and how good of a lover are they? Why don't we stay over at one another's place on occasion to test the waters a little? Are we ready to live together?*

These are the clear standards by which *Cosmo*, Facebook, and Hollywood judge dating relationships, but let me be clear: They are pathetic pathways to commitment, horrible benchmarks to gauge relational quality and stability, and often lead to relational self-sabotage. Don't adopt them or be taken in by their salacious promises.

Now, back to the FAQs and their answers, which are rooted in wisdom and will help you manage each stage of dating. Hold them close and remember that w*hen kids predate a new couple, marriage is a package deal. If you can't marry the package, or aren't ready to embrace all that comes with the package, don't marry the person.*

Q: If We're in Love, Why Should We Wait to Get Married?

A: Don't rush dating and don't rush a decision to marry. Time is your friend. Slow the pace of your dating and fill it with purposeful conversation so you can explore how well your life trajectories might merge. Avoid being driven by surface-level infatuation, and instead look deep into the mirror to examine the person you are and the person they are.

Time will help you to see whether you and the other person are a fit not just on the surface, but to the core. Time will make known transparency or hiding, authenticity or façade, integrity or falsehood. Time will reveal what you don't like about each other and whether you can problem-solve through it (couples who break up even once during dating are four times more likely to have relationship difficulties than couples who don't[4]). And time will reveal whether your extended families can merge or if cohesiveness is unlikely; if both of you are parents, whether your parenting styles can complement or compete; and whether each parent is strong enough to lead their children through the transition to a new family. Don't rush past the children and their need for reliable, consistent nurturing from you. And let the pace of your coupleness be influenced by—not controlled by—the leanings, longings, anxieties, and openness of the children.

> **Timing Issues**
>
> In general, men are open to dating more quickly after a death or divorce than are women, and both are ready to date before their kids want them to.

Don't dismiss time; she is trying to help you. Listen to her.

Q: How Do I Proceed Without Feeling Overwhelmed?

A: If you are feeling overwhelmed at this point, you may be trying to comprehend and master every stage even before you get there. Instead of trying to get your hands around all of them at once, try to focus on the stage you are in and trust God to help you manage it well. Only then do you have to deal with the next stage—and God will be there, too. It's a little like trusting God with life.

Do you know how God gives directions? If you were to ask me how to get from my house to the local Walmart, I would give you step-by-step instructions. For example, I might say drive southwest in front of my house on London Court toward Liberty. Turn left at the stop sign. Then, curve through our neighborhood until you come to Continental Parkway; turn left. Continue east two-tenths of a mile till turning left onto Coulter Road. Walmart will be half a mile on your left. But that's not how God gives directions.

In his book *Experiencing God*, Henry Blackaby says that God doesn't give us directions that way; he only gives us the next set of instructions and then waits for us to obey. He might, for example, say, "Drive southwest on London Court," and then stop talking. We, of course, then anxiously ask, "And then what, God?" He responds, "Don't worry about that, just drive that direction on London Court." "Yeah, but God, I need to know what follows that so I can get prepared." "I'm not interested in you bring prepared." He smiles. "I'm interested in you trusting me to know the way; I'll give you more when it's best." I don't know about you, but God's direction-giving style really frustrates me! My need to know—and be in control—is too high for this to be comfortable. But that's exactly why God does it that way; he wants to deepen my trust, not my knowing.

To keep from being overwhelmed by the dating stages, give yourself permission to not know how to master the next step. Trust God to lead you through when you get there. In the meantime, trust him with the stage you're in now.

Q: Given the Magnitude of This Process, Should I Do Myself and My Kids a Favor and Wait Till the Kids Are Gone Before Dating?

A: I don't know how old your kids are, but honestly, it's worth considering. Essentially, what dating and marriage creates is a competition of emotional attachment and priorities between you, your children, and your partner/spouse. When it's just you and the kids, the attachments are clear and your priority is parenting.

When you begin to date, you gradually shift your time, attention, and priority to the new love; at marrige you make the ultimate shift to "forsake all others till death do you part." Of course, this doesn't mean you abandon or neglect your children after marriage, but it does mean that your decisions are more firmly rooted in your companion than in your children. No wonder kids feel left out and in competition with their parent's new love. This also helps us understand why many children who at one point were in favor of their parent dating, and might have even encouraged them to marry, later begin protesting a parent's marriage.

Whether you have kids or not, please know that dating and marriage when kids are present is a gain for you but initially a loss for the kids (until family bonding takes place—which can take years—and then becomes a gain for the kids, too). There's no way around this truth. Single parents ask me all the time, "Can I find a new love and not make my kids feel displaced?" I respond, "Unless your children are very small and your ex-spouse is cooperative and open to you remarrying, probably not."

Melanie wrote to me, "I seriously dated a man for a while, and my children did not like him or his children at all. While I didn't allow my children to break up the relationship, I did spend much time asking them specifically what their concerns were and addressed them. I feel it's critical to pay attention to a child's response." Jackie said, "If the child has outbursts because of a new partner, it should be talked through to find out if it's just jealousy or something worse. A parent may have to take a step back from dating and let their child know that they are not being replaced." Melanie is applying a great deal of wisdom. A child's jealousy is the result of the traumatic losses they have already experienced (e.g., death of a parent or divorce, and all the changes since). They don't want any more loss—and when you shift your energy toward someone else, it is another loss.

This is less of a concern for very young children (preschool age) because they aren't as aware of life before and after the new stepparent. They are also more open to new people in their lives. Children between the ages of ten and fifteen seem, on the other hand, to have the most difficulty making space for a stepparent, stepsiblings, and all the transition that comes with them.[5] Waiting to date till the children are grown and on their own avoids the competition of attachment at a developmentally significant time of the children's lives—and it's worth considering. It allows you to focus on raising your children and preparing them for adulthood; it allows them to deal with what is already on their plate without more emotionally draining transitions being added on.

Now, I realize that remaining single in order to focus on raising your children is a challenging thought, and not many will be drawn to it. I'm just suggesting it's worth prayerful consideration. Marriage is a blessing to the part of your heart that longs for partnership. However, remaining single is a blessing to the parental part of your heart and carries a blessing for your children, as well.

One more thought before leaving this subject. If you wait till the kids are launched from your home, please do not assume that an empty-nest blended family will be adjustment free. Every stepfamily, no matter what the age of the children, has significant transitions to manage. For example, stepparents of adult stepchildren don't struggle because they're trying to figure out how to discipline the children; they struggle because they still feel like outsiders to the family's history, traditions, and rituals. And the

> ## I Chose to Wait
>
> "I chose to wait it out. I had two very angry children who were acting out after the divorce. People told me for years I was wasting my life—that if I brought a man into their lives, it would help them not act out so much. I turned fifty this year. I raised them for fourteen years on my own. They are adults now; the youngest of my four is twenty. Now I can think about dating. I am trusting God to bring a man into my life if that is his will."

Take the Couple Checkup

The Couple Checkup is an online assessment of twenty relationship areas significant for dating, engaged, and married couples. Based on over thirty years of research, the Checkup is a highly respected relationship tool used by marriage experts around the world. Get one free Individual Report at www.smartstepfamilies.com by using the voucher code provided inside the back cover of this book. This code also provides a 50 percent discount if you upgrade to the full couple report (available after you have completed your free Individual Profile).

stepchildren, even as adults, worry about how incorporating the new stepparent into their lives will impact their relationship with the other biological parent, etc. (To learn more, read *The Smart Stepmom* and *The Smart Stepdad*, in which I address adult stepfamilies and their adjustment issues.) The upside, though, is that these transitions don't occur during the important developmental years of a child's life and are, therefore, less negatively impactful. Because the transition to becoming a new family occurs when everyone is more mature, stepfamily adjustment does seem to be easier for most families. That adds one more reason to consider waiting till the kids are gone.

Q: Does It Matter How Long You Date Before Marriage?

A: No, and yes. Just as I used to tell people not to date for two years after their divorce or death of their spouse, I used to tell couples they should date for at least two years before deciding to marry. That was before Dr. David Olson and I conducted the largest study of single parents getting ready to marry their partners. We studied the profiles of over 50,000 couples and published our practical findings in the book *The Remarriage Checkup*. By the way, you can take the Couple Checkup, a similar profile to the one we used in our research, and assess your relationship. It's a great way to get an objective perspective on the health of your relationship, which helps you make more informed decisions about the future.

In our study, we discovered what predicts great remarriage relationships (defined as a marriage in which either spouse or both have been previously married) and we learned that the length of time a couple dates does not predict couple relationship quality. That is, couples who dated a few months were just as likely to have a high- or low-quality relationship as couples who dated a few years. In other words, it's possible to have a high-quality dating relationship in just a few months. But that doesn't mean it's wise to rapidly get married.

As I have already stated, when children are involved, a marriage between the two of you is not just between the two of you. How long you date matters significantly to kids and greatly impacts your future blended family. Let me remind you of the central point of this book: Coupleness does not equal familyness. You might have a quality couple relationship within six months, but that doesn't mean your family will do well or that your marriage can't be pulled apart by conflicts over the children, ex-spouses, or an ex-mother-in-law. Learning to steer and balance a tandem (two-person) bicycle is tough, but it's not as challenging as bringing the Queen Mary into port. They are two different processes.

In the next chapter I'll explain in more detail what this family dynamic is all about, but for now hear this: Even if you are ready to get engaged or marry, it may not be wise to do so until the family is ready. Someone who asks "How long should we date?" is usually already thinking about marriage, and they are hoping they can get permission to jump in. That's why you have to remember that time is your friend—not only for your relationship, but for the needs of the kids. Children need much more time than couples, and you only shoot yourself in the foot if you ignore their timing.

If You Don't Have Kids

If you don't have children, it can be difficult to give appropriate consideration to the openness and readiness of the children of the person you're dating. It may feel like the children are holding your relationship hostage. Instead, put on compassion for what your presence is requiring of them, and be patient with their timing.

Ron, are you saying that kids get to determine when the couple marries? Not at all. But it's wise to be influenced by their degree of openness; only a fool will ignore how significant their feelings really are to becoming a blended family.

When a Parent Is Deceased

Quick dating (less than one year) and a quick remarriage (less than two years after death) can be perceived by children as a low-value statement regarding the parent who has died. This feels offensive and casts a negative shadow on the new relationship.

For example, teenage and adult children often scowl at a parent's marriage when it follows a short courtship. One man, even fifteen years into his remarriage, found himself repeatedly trying to convince his two adult daughters that he really loved his new wife. Less than one year after his first wife died of cancer, the couple had met and married within six weeks. His daughters decided as soon as the wedding was announced that there was no way their father loved this woman. "How could he?" they insisted. "Mom has only been gone a little while and he doesn't even know this new person. He's deceived." From that time forward, they closed themselves and would not accept the marriage or their stepmother. Time matters.

Q: If We Decide to Marry, Will Faithfully Following These Stages Guarantee Us a Successful Blended Family?

A: Of course not. There are no guarantees in life. None of us can anticipate what life will bring our way or what will be required of us when we get there. That's why we need commitment.

Discerning your fit for partnership and becoming a family is the task of dating. Commitment in marriage is what helps you live out this discerning belief and turn it into reality. People often think if they didn't choose well, they can't be happily married. I'm not so sure. Don't get me wrong—choosing well matters, but so does the commitment made by each person once they decide to marry. How else do the arranged marriages of many cultures around the world last? Commitment glues the couple together and gives God a chance to really go to work on their selfishness, mistaken expectations, pride, and immature views of intimacy.

Here's God's master plan for us: He asks us to vow to love, honor, and cherish, and then he uses life to teach us what we committed ourselves to. And that's when God grows us up—as we learn how to live out our vows. Commitment is important because it gives us the chance to make mistakes while learning what God wants us to learn. Said another way, commitment is important because of what we do after we make the commitment; the power is not so much in making the decision, but in the actions we take to uphold the decision and the lessons learned along the way. No one, no matter how well they dated, knows what marriage will require of them. In 1986 when I married Nan, I had no earthly idea what parts of me would have to change in order to love her and live with her—and neither did she. God is continually growing us up, teaching us how to love one another, and molding us into the image of Christ so we can in turn deepen our love for one another. It's a marvelous, wondrous—and painful—process! And only those who are willing to die to self and submit themselves to the discipling process of marriage receive its rewards.

> **Dating Too Long**
>
> Couples who date five years or longer are significantly more likely to have lower-quality relationships. We theorize that couples who can't pull the trigger on marriage after five years of dating have some barriers they cannot overcome, including significant levels of fear (see chapter 4). They get stuck and just can't move forward (and probably shouldn't).

By the way, this is why cohabitation doesn't work. I'll say much more about this in chapter 7, but it's important to say now that cohabitation is not commitment, neither does it tell you whether your relationship would work if you made a commitment. I once coached a single parent who had been dating a man for three years. He was ready to get married, but she just couldn't pull the trigger. When I asked if she wanted a guarantee that the marriage would last before becoming engaged, she said, "Absolutely. That's why we're living together instead; I want to know if this will work."

With much compassion for her fear I replied, "But cohabitation isn't marriage—and until you make a full commitment to each other, you'll never know what you'd be willing to do for one another. Right now you're just dipping your toe in the deep end of the pool; you can feel the temperature, but you'll never know if you can swim until you throw your whole self in." There are no guarantees in life or relationships—there is always risk. Either choose risk or don't; when the time comes, choose commitment or don't. But don't sit on the side of the pool with one foot in the water telling everyone you're swimming.

FINAL THOUGHTS

Consumer daters want guarantees. "I won't purchase this marriage until I know my partner will love me as only my true soul mate can and is everything I want them to be—and will last 100,000 miles or fifty years, whichever comes first." How absurd. Instead of being a consumer who selfishly purposes in dating to find the one person you believe will serve your needs, purpose instead:

- to make sure *you* are being the right person for God; and
- to follow Christ, and while you do, look around for another Christ-follower who shares your heart, interests, life objectives, background, parenting style, and vision for family. Once you find them, walk in faith together.

Discussion Questions

1. People with repeated failed relationships often make the following mistakes. Which are you or the person you are dating guilty of?

   - They don't have a purpose in dating.

   - They lack an intentional process to their dating.

   - They don't have an appreciation for the complexity of dating in a crowd.

   - They don't take the children's needs and feelings into consideration enough.

   - They don't realize that the growing connections between the children and future stepparents or stepsiblings established during dating may shift toward distance and conflict after the wedding.

2. What does a consumer attitude in dating look like? What should you look for to identify that attitude in yourself or someone else?

3. God is always using the circumstances of our lives to grow us up. Digest these questions:

   - Are you open to what God is teaching you about him in your singleness?

   - Are you pursuing him as much as he is pursuing you?

   - Is your singleness helping you to see him more clearly and trust him more deeply, or are you instead telling him what he should be doing for you?

   - Are you open to maturing in this season of life, or do you assume that you need marriage to be fulfilled?

4. I proposed three purposes for dating in this chapter. Discuss each and what it would look like to live out each in a dating relationship.

- Discern if, together, you and this other person can walk humbly with God with a common heart, faith, value system, and approach to life.

- Discern if you can love the person sacrificially without reservation, and trust that they will do the same for you.

- Discern if the children involved in your union would be graced by your common commitment to the Lord and combined families.

5. If you are dating a single parent, how would you know if they were not giving enough consideration to the needs of their children as it relates to dating you?

6. Society has many ambiguous, simplistic, and shallow benchmarks for gauging the status of dating relationships. How have these or others influenced your dating in the past: Is this person good-looking and do I get points just for standing beside them? Are they wealthy or do they at least have the potential to become wealthy? Do they hang out with the right people? Are they sexually experienced (because I don't want to be with a novice)? Have we had sex yet and how good of a lover are they? Why don't we stay over at one another's place on occasion to test the waters a little? Am I ready to move in with them, and what happens when we live together?

7. Review the Dating Process FAQs beginning on page 34. Discuss the implications for you and the kids.

Chapter 2

Mirror, Mirror on the Wall: Am I Ready to Date?

Before Mom met Larry, she cried a lot. She was worried that all of us kids would go off and live our own lives and she'd be all alone. (Corey's mom, a well-educated professional, met and married a man in six weeks' time. They were divorced one and a half years later.)

Corey, age 17

Are you ready to love again? Are you ready to risk again? And if you think you are, how would you recognize being vulnerable, like Corey's mom, to an unhealthy relationship?

When love requires a lot, most of us rethink—at least on some level—our willingness to give. When love requires some, a few will bow out, but most stay in the game. When love requires very little, nearly everyone thinks they are ready for it.

For years I've jokingly referred to dating as "The Big Lie." Each person puts their best foot forward in an attempt to be liked by the other. He will open the car door for her every time they go out; she will take the time to watch his favorite sporting event (even though she'd rather do anything other than that). He will plan creative dates and offer small gestures to show her he cares; she will overlook his annoying personal habits and make excuses for his decision to wear certain out-of-fashion clothes. He will unfriend old girlfriends from his Facebook page, and the only pictures she will post of herself are ones taken before she gained a few pounds. The Big Lie—it is the nature of the dating game.

Please understand, it's not that these people are really trying to deceive each other. They just want the other person to like them, so they present themselves in the best manner possible. For a few months at least, this best-foot-forward approach creates a near fantasy dating experience that doesn't require a great deal of sacrifice from dating partners. Because everyone is on their best behavior, love is natural, invigorating, energizing, and hope producing. It is easy and requires little in the way of emotional trust, vulnerability, or an intermingling of one another's lives (things like children and parenting, extended family, traditions, values, and lifestyle choices).

Who would think they weren't ready for that?

Here's the point: Most people during the pre-dating and early dating stages are focused on finding the right person and then impressing the socks off them, when what they ought to focus on is *being* the right person. Dating starts not by looking outward, but by looking in.

This and the next chapter will help you to do just that—look carefully into the mirror so you can become the right person and assess your readiness for dating. This will create a more presentable and attractive *you* should you encounter someone of interest.

DEATH AND DIVORCE RECOVERY . . . REALLY?

Pre-dating preparation usually begins with single parents having to recover from something: a death, a divorce (or relationship breakup), or some other significant loss. But you are deceived if you think that once you've "recovered," you've moved past that pain forever.

Cassandra wrote to us at Smart Stepfamilies and shared how her church divorce recovery program had been helpful to her. "I think healing before remarriage is the most important thing a person can do for themselves and their children. I went through a DivorceCare class, and my current husband did a divorce recovery program at his church that helped him deal with his divorce. These programs helped us make changes that needed to be made, and have blessed our marriage, as well."

I am a strong believer in divorce recovery and support ministries that help widowed persons move through their grief. (For example, I highly recommend the DivorceCare and GriefShare programs.) These support ministries help people learn how to manage their grief in a healthy way, give them perspective on how their marriage came to an end, and help them take responsibility for how they contributed to a dissolved marriage. Recovery programs also provide stability at a time of emotional upheaval through practical

> **Knowing Yourself**
>
> How vulnerable are you to a dating partner's best-foot-forward behaviors? How easily are you drawn in to the fantasy?

counsel, encouraging relationships with others in the group, and a godly perspective on forgiveness, healing, and managing anger.

But in spite of all the good these programs bring to our lives, I have to ask the question: Does anyone *fully* recover?

To recover is to get back or regain a normal position or condition.[1] Really? Is that possible after tragedy strikes? It hasn't happened for me.

Taken

As I write, it is two days before Father's Day, a day that I used to cherish but now dread with every fiber of my being. In

February of 2009 my wife, Nan, and I went to a movie. It was a Saturday night and we just needed to get away from the kids and refresh ourselves. We went to see the movie *Taken*, starring Liam Neeson. The movie is about a father whose daughter is abducted—that is, taken—for the purpose of child trafficking. As any good father would do, Liam Neeson hunts down the men responsible and saves the day. After a fun, wild ride at the theater, we returned home to find our middle son, Connor, complaining of a headache. Little did we know that at that very hour Connor was being taken. We gave him an ibuprofen and sent him to bed, confident he would feel better in the morning. He didn't.

An MRSA staph infection had contaminated his body and was systematically destroying his lungs. Over the next ten days we journeyed up and down steep mountains of hope and fear, and spiraled through narrow passages of prayer until finally descending into the valley of the shadow of death. Connor was gone from this life. Taken.

There is no recovery from this. There is only surviving and getting through. That may sound pessimistic or without faith to you, but I have talked with enough counselors and grieving parents who are decades further down the road than us to know that until heaven we will never go back to "normal." A good, long look in the mirror has shown us that our life is forever changed and time now falls into the categories of *before* and *after*.

- Before: I never once prayed for daily bread. I prayed for early retirement.

  After: I'm learning what it is to pray for daily survival and to wait on the Lord's provision for this moment—to be still and know that he is God.

- Before: I prayed "if the Lord wills" such-and-such will happen, just like the book of James says to do.

After: I realize that I didn't mean it when I said that. I said "if the Lord wills," but I never gave it an honest thought that my plans for life wouldn't really come about. I was smitten with the illusion of control. If I just worked hard enough, prayed hard enough, lived right enough, things would pretty much work out. Now when I say "tomorrow I will do this or that," I don't have any illusion that it will really happen . . . unless the Lord wills. My illusions have been ruptured.

- Before: Nan and I thought we knew what it was to be and have friends.

  After: We have discovered the faithfulness of a few amazing friends who are willing to walk through darkness with us, day after day, year after year, even when we can't be for them who we once were. We have also learned that lots of other "friends" can't handle our pain—and won't handle our pain. Never before had we experienced social isolation and loneliness until we entered the valley of death.

- Before: I thought a bad day was the flu, a flat tire, or a flight delay.

  After: My definition of a bad day has been recalibrated. Watching my wife dig her fingernails into our son's grave while screaming "I want my son back," or helplessly standing by as one of Connor's brothers is submerged night after night in the fear that another family member will die, now qualify as a bad day.

- Before: Sunday was a time of family connection, worship, and celebrating our Lord.

  After: Sunday is often the worst day of the week and worship the worst hour. Songs without Connor's voice, the memory of his casket at the front of the auditorium, the feeling of abandonment by those we thought were friends, etc., make worship a time of confusion and agony.

- Before: I thought trust and faith were the antidotes to pain.

After: I've realized that the train I now travel sits on two rails: the left is sadness (deep, deep sadness) and the right wonderful memories. The left is anguish, the right hope. The left anger, the right trust. The left sorrow, the right peace in the arms of Jesus. Neither rail invalidates the other. Neither excludes the other. They coexist. I now know that faith doesn't end grief, and the hope of heaven still allows room for asking why. I travel these two rails, side by side, – on an unstoppable train . . . till Jesus comes.

My guess is that by now you've realized (for yourself or the person you are dating) that your life is also forever changed, that there is no full recovery from the tragedy of death or divorce, and that you, too, are riding on the same train. Yes, my tragedy and pain are different from yours, but even still, your tragic loss has changed you. You have a before and after story, too. Just look in the mirror.

- Before: You were sure you had found the one and only love of your life.

  After: You realized infatuation stole your discernment, and you married someone you didn't know, someone who eventually became your enemy. And now you don't trust your decisions.

- Before: You dreamed of growing old with someone.

  After: You discovered that life is fragile, and not even the righteous can assume they are protected from death.

- Before: You had friends, lots of friends, who welcomed you and made you feel at home.

  After: As friends took sides, you lost a few, and the ones who remained soon faded into their married-couple world. You ended up alone and in search of new friends.

- Before: You believed that if you love and serve someone, they will be faithful to you.

After: A sight, sound, or smell instantly transports you back to the time when your knees buckled under the weight of betrayal. And now you doubt if anyone really keeps their promises.

- Before: You were confident to take on life. Your marriage and home life supported your work, interests, and ambitions.

  After: You are lucky to stay ahead of the bills. Ambition is dead, and you are socially withdrawn and embarrassed about your life situation.

- Before: You worshiped God with a blind trust and questioned others who got angry with him.

  After: For a season, you cursed God to his face, felt justified in doing so, and refused to open your mouth in praise. With your anger now subsiding, you are again open to your Father but still baffled at why he would let you and your children suffer so much.

Tragedy changes us forever. Sometimes for the better and sometimes for the worse, but do not be mistaken, it changes us forever. One of the biggest mistakes I have seen countless singles make is assuming that because they or their dating partner graduated from a support ministry, there no longer exists a residue of pain in their heart. Because the intensity of pain has lifted does not mean that you have learned everything you needed to learn or have moved past your pain. Sadness, pain, and doubt will coexist with faith, at some level, throughout life. You are forever different—in both positive and negative ways:

> **Kids Talk**
>
> "How could God have let this happen to my family? Does he really care about me? Can I trust him to be there for us?"

- Positive: You are more self-reliant now. Your previous husband left you with nothing but the clothes on your back. At first you were petrified, but by God's hand you found a job,

If You Are Dating a Single Parent

Take time to listen to the "before and after" story of your dating partner and their children (if they are open to sharing it). The more you know about how profoundly their lives have changed, the more informed your choices will be about the relationship and the more compassionate you will be to their fears and hesitations.

a house, and friends who came through for you over and over. You not only survived, you learned that you have the ability to find your way.

Negative: You are more self-reliant now. Coming to depend on God and yourself was tough, but now that you're there, leaning on another man for financial support is downright scary.

• Positive: You are a more involved dad now. Picking up the pieces after your wife died wasn't easy, but you did it. What was most difficult was engaging your children on an emotional level that you had previously relegated to their mother. You had to find a way to touch their hearts—and you did.

Negative: You are a more involved dad now. Not only did you learn to hold your children's hearts, you cherish doing so. Now that you're dating, your girlfriend is moving in on your territory. Most people assume it would be a relief for you, but you just feel threatened—and guilty that your kids are losing a part of you.

If you are a single parent who has been through a death or divorce, as you ponder how your life has changed, here are three points to chew on. First, humble yourself enough to admit that you are changed. Real recovery does not transport you back to being the person you were before the tragedy; it incorporates who you were with who you have had to become. Be open to discovering this and integrating these various parts of you.

Second, keep in mind that your kids are different, too. As I've written in each of my other books, children never recover from the death of a parent or parental divorce. They live the rest of their lives in the shadow of that event. Yes, they are resilient and quite capable of adapting to the new normal of their family, but no, they don't stop wondering about what might have been, wishing that broken relationships would mend, or grieving the multitude of losses that keep accumulating since the death or divorce.

Third, dating has a way of showing you that the growth you gained from your recovery work was sufficient to being single, but not sufficient for contributing to an "us." Just because you have done some recovery work doesn't mean you or your children are ready for new relationships. Take one step at a time and don't be surprised if dating reveals a hurt or pain you didn't know existed.

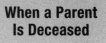

When a Parent Is Deceased

If your former spouse died, you may not be wrestling with shame, but you may have regrets. Let God affirm your value in spite of your failings, and don't try to make up for those regrets in a new relationship.

Here is something worth considering: A parent who has turned a blind eye to how they or their children have been changed by the past will make repeated dating mistakes. They will run over dating partners, fall short in caring for their children, and make foolish decisions about remarriage. A buried past is usually buried alive—and easily resurrected. Better to carry the past with you, reflect, and humbly listen.

GOD'S MIRROR

There's another mirror that I want to encourage you to look into. It's the mirror in which you see yourself as God sees you.

You are his chosen child, beloved and cherished. No matter where you've been or what you've done, he loves you. I share this because many of the divorced persons I've worked with over the years have struggled with tremendous guilt and spiritual shame. Even if the divorce wasn't their decision, they feel unworthy, perhaps even second class.

There are two things to think about, I tell them. First, remember that God is really good at forgiveness. He's been doing it a long time and he took great pain in making a way for grace to be available to—yes, even divorced people (tongue in cheek)! So let him forgive you; embrace his grace.

Second, remind yourself that while you can't earn his grace, God does call you to obedience. The reason he wants you to be obedient, by the way, is not because "I said so." We parents sometimes give this response to our children when we don't know what else to say. It's as if we are saying, "I and the rule are one, so do it." No, God invites our obedience because he knows the good he has in store for us when we live a certain way. His statutes are meant to provide for us, protect us, and mature us. There's a gift in the command—we just have to trust that his loving heart is working on our behalf through the precept.

Pursuing Spiritual Blessing

If you were to fall in love with someone and marry them, would you have the blessing of God? Would you have the blessing of your local church family? Both of these questions are of the utmost importance for the divorced person. If you have been widowed, Scripture is clear that you are free to marry. Paul actually encourages widows to remain single so their dedication to the Lord can be undeterred; however, if remaining single with sexual purity isn't your gifting, Paul says, as long as you marry a believer, you are free to remarry (see 1 Corinthians 7:8–9, 39). But if you are divorced, questions about your freedom to marry with God's blessing and approval are critical.

Pursue the Smile of God. Every bride wants her father to give her away with his blessing. What every Christian couple hopes is for God to in effect do the same, that is, to "give them away" to each other with his blessing. Starting the journey of marriage with God's smile on you is to begin on the right foot. Everyone wants that. To take the first step while hiding in shame casts a shadow on the legitimacy of the marriage. No one wants that. Therefore, it is important to seek God's will for your life as it relates to marriage. I believe the high calling of Scripture for divorced persons is to reconcile their original marriages if at all possible.[2] God created marriage in part to reflect the oneness of the Trinity and be a testimony to the world of selfless love. When a marriage dissolves, unity is broken and the testimony lost. But how much more is God glorified when a divorced couple reconciles their marriage and transforms it into a God-honoring, mutually serving in love kind of marriage!

Now, having said that restoration of a separated or dissolved marriage is near to the heart of God, I want to acknowledge that this won't be likely in many situations and wouldn't be prudent in others. For example, returning to an unbelieving partner or restoring an abusive marriage would not bring glory to God unless there was radical repentance. The fundamental nature of such a marriage would have to be drastically different in order for a reconciliation to reflect God's purposes in marriage.[3] In addition, if your ex has remarried already, reconciliation is not possible (in fact, Scripture teaches against them divorcing their new spouse to return to you; see Deuteronomy 24:1–4).

There are many other Scriptures and scenarios we could examine, but my point is this: Don't move on to another marital partner without first giving serious consideration to the calling of reconciliation. Instead, explore with a trusted spiritual advisor, pastor, or ministry (e.g., www.reconcilinggodsway.org) the choices or actions you may have available to you as it relates to your former spouse[4] and what the Bible teaches about this matter.[5]

SLOW YOUR GAZE

The next chapter will explore a number of other aspects of your readiness to date, but slow down, don't turn the page just yet. This chapter started your examination of self with what I consider to be the two most important facets of readiness: (1) the impact loss has had on you, and (2) your willingness to surrender to God's direction regarding divorce and remarriage. Both of these are vital and should not be quickly passed by. If you are divorced and already in a dating relationship with someone you really like, you may have skipped the last section. You don't want anyone suggesting you might need to reconsider the relationship for spiritual reasons (and if you do feel that irritation right now, it might be your conscience telling you to do just that). Or perhaps you are running so fast from your past, you have never taken the time to reflect on how it has changed you or your children. You must stop. Slow your gaze in front of the mirror and take a good long look at yourself. You won't be able to outrun these two facets of your life.

Let me put it another way—you can pay now or pay later. For over a decade I have specialized in stepfamily therapy and working with remarried couples, and one thing experience has taught me is that people who ignore these components of their life often pay a price for them later when they have a new marriage, new family, and much more on the line. Had they dealt with it before dating, they might not have even married who they married. Now they and their kids are paying the price. Pray through these aspects of your life. Ask for insight and be open to what the mirror—and the Holy Spirit—shows you.

Discussion Questions

1. Dating can be "The Big Lie." Look back over your previous dating experiences and examine how easy it is to fall prey to the best-foot-forward fantasy that early dating creates.

2. What concrete steps have you taken to bring healing from your past losses? If you haven't participated in any structured opportunity so far (e.g., counseling or divorce recovery program), why not?

3. List your befores and afters. How has your loss recalibrated your attitudes, parenting, and outlook on life?

   • If you are dating someone who has also experienced loss, do you know how they are different? If not, listen to their story and find out.

4. How are your kids (and/or partner's kids) different? What are their befores and afters?

5. Regarding a previous relationship/marriage, what regret, guilt, or shame lingers for you?

6. If you are divorced, I encourage you not to move on to another marital partner without first giving serious consideration to Scripture's calling of reconciliation. What implications does this have for you or the person you are dating?

7. Slowing your gaze is about giving yourself time to hear what the Holy Spirit has for you in this season of your life. What steps can you take to slow down and not rush into a new relationship?

Chapter 3

Ready or Not, Here I Come: The Readiness Factors

When I first became single, everyone told me to wait at least two years to date, and I laughed at them; I now realize what good advice that was.

Sheri, single parent

As you continue to look in the mirror, let me dispel a myth right now. The idea that either you or a dating partner is definitively ready or not ready for another relationship is misguided. It's not a black or white, either/or situation. It's more of a continuum of gray. For example, you might think after a period of self-examination and counsel that you are ready to meet someone. But all it takes is a first date for you to realize that you are ready for only casual dating, not a serious relationship.

Let's take the pressure off right now. Stop worrying about whether you're ready to date, and stop trying to discern whether your kids are ready for you to date yet (we'll talk more about that in the next chapter). No one but God knows the answer to these questions! And unless he writes a message to you on the wall (your Facebook wall or otherwise), I suggest you reflect on the following readiness markers, and then perhaps try dating and see what happens. Yeah, that's right, try dating. Sometimes that's the only way to expose readiness factors you didn't know to attend to. As you date, continually reflect and listen to what you are experiencing and learning about yourself, your children, your dating partner, and the "us" that is being developed between you.

EMOTIONAL READINESS

Have you ever watched a celebrity interview on TV and thought, *How can that person be so unaware of how strange they sound? They really think they are making sense. How can someone be that arrogant, self-centered, or nearsighted?* What is missing in that person is the ability to look in the mirror, to see themselves objectively, for who they really are.

Look in the Emotional Readiness Mirror

Part of what keeps us humble before God is the ability to look in the mirror. It will also help you consider your emotional readiness for dating. What are your internal drives at this season of your life? What strong emotions persist? Emotions like guilt, fear, loneliness, or unhappiness do not create fertile soil for growing healthy relationships, and discontentment breeds vulnerability and poor discernment. To what degree do these emotions exist in your life?

Regularly I ask single-agains "How do you know if you are ready to date?" Sheri shared, "In order to be ready to date again, you really need to have come to terms with what went wrong in the marriage and accept your part of the blame and responsibility for it. You should be at a place where you want to make changes in your own life so that your next relationship is much better. Also, make sure enough time has passed for you or the person you are dating. When I first became single, everyone told me to wait at least two years to date, and I laughed at them; I now realize what good advice that was." I like Sheri's willingness to look in the mirror.

Kerry, a divorced mom, emphasized to women the importance of becoming self-reliant. "First, you truly have to be over your relationship with your previous husband in all aspects; no one wants you to constantly compare them to your ex-spouse. You have to realize that you do not *need* a man, as you will choose ineffectively if you are needy and are just looking for someone to take care of you and your children. You must have the financial means to care for yourself and children without needing anyone else. Woman, be strong and learn to stand on your own two feet. You can take care of you and your children with self-confidence, drive, and attitude. No is never an option!" Obviously Kerry is suggesting that if you see neediness in the mirror, you aren't ready to date.

> **If You Are Not a Parent**
>
> Singles who have never been married or don't have any children can "need" to be married, too. It is a yellow caution light if either of you has a strong urgency to get married.

And then there was this response from the other side of the fence. "Regretful from Canada" anonymously wrote my ministry, sharing her already married blended family perspective. Unfortunately for her, she wasn't able to look in the mirror until it was too late.

My husband and I are both in second marriages, but I wish I had never remarried. I have two young teenagers and he has a five-year-old he has never seen but talks to every few weeks. I remarried after being on my own for three years. I now realize that I married again because I was terrified of being alone and desperately wanted to have a healthy family for my children. Unfortunately, my second husband cannot relate to my children and sees them only as a duty. In fact, all aspects of family life seem to be a chore for him. This causes tremendous tension between us. I fought for my first marriage for many years until it was torn from me. I have no more fight left in me. I try to give it to God, but only find temporary peace. I have been thinking about leaving for over a year now. My children have tried to relate and bond with him, but have been pushed away. We have seen counselors together and separately. Initially I was sad that I had made another mistake, but now I am getting angry at myself for being so needy back then and at him for not being who I want him to be. Divorcing this time wouldn't seem to be wrong because I wouldn't be tearing apart a family—we aren't a family.

It is easy to hear Regretful's pain and defeat. She doesn't even classify her situation as a family. (I would, however, because she and her husband made a covenant promise; her family is worthy of being saved, it just needs much improvement.) But what is worthy of our attention is her observation that loneliness and worry for her children closed her eyes to wise discernment about marriage and becoming a blended family. She didn't take her loneliness and worry seriously and didn't examine her emotional readiness thoroughly. As a result, she found herself in a regretful situation.

Marital Amnesia

Definition: The willingness to date again even after a painful divorce or spouse's death.

1. loss of relational memory due usually to loneliness, fear, discontent, or the desire to climb out of the pit of pain

2. a gap in one's memory

3. the selective overlooking or ignoring of events or acts that are not favorable or useful to one's purpose or position of getting into another relationship

Relax in Your Aloneness

As I stated in the introduction, God made us to be relational beings. When without a companion, we will feel alone. That loneliness must be acknowledged and managed so it doesn't place blinders on your eyes. Loneliness might be one of the strongest causes of marital amnesia, which fools people into believing they are ready for a new relationship and causes them to minimize the complexity of forming a blended family.

So what's the prescription for loneliness? Relax in your aloneness. I know that sounds crazy, but let me explain. Finding the ability with God's help to be still in your loneliness is not a remedy for loneliness—you will still feel lonely—but if you learn to trust God with your loneliness, meet it head on, and manage it responsibly, it won't dictate or drive your decisions.

> **Kids Talk**
>
> "My dad tells me to wait for the right girl to come along and not get impatient. But he can't live without a woman in his life. That's a little hypocritical, don't you think?"

Rebound relationships are a good example of loneliness at the steering wheel. After the loss of a significant relationship, it's common to feel as if you've fallen into a pit of pain. One reason people rebound into a new relationship is that it functions as a ladder to help them climb out of their pain. Unfortunately, the drive to get out of the pit is so strong that it blinds people to the weaknesses of the ladder and the fact that they are using this person to medicate their pain. In the end, the weak ladder—a pseudo-relationship at best—crumbles, and you (and your children) fall again into the pit of pain.

To truly move out of your pain, you must first sit in it. You must recognize your hurt, your loneliness, your despair and call out to God for help as you walk through it. This is an excruciating process for many, especially those who have had divorce thrust upon them, but there's no other healthy way to manage the pit and keep it from creating vulnerability in your life. You can't sidestep the pit.

How will you know when you are relaxing in your aloneness? When you recognize your loneliness but don't *need* to find another person; when you can choose to enjoy the good parts of your life without feeling that they could be better if you just had a person to share them with; when you aren't overwhelmed by a profound sense of failure or inadequacy; and when fear, guilt, and discontent don't control your decisions or push you to search for a partner, but you instead devote time to exploring and understanding your fear, guilt, and discontent. Then you are relaxing in your aloneness.

Since losing my son Connor, I can't tell you how isolated our family has been (most folks don't like to hang around grieving parents) or how many times I've been tempted to quit my job, sell the house, and disappear on the other side of the planet somewhere. After a few years of continuous heavy sorrow, sometimes you just want to chuck it all and quit life. The temptation to rapidly climb out of the pit of pain is very real for me.

But where would that leave me? In denial, emotionally lost, spiritually vulnerable, and addicted to the agent of my quick fix, I suspect. So instead of letting my pain dictate my journey out of the pit, I've decided to sit in the pit and feel it. Every single bit of it. Yes, I cut myself a break every now and then and allow myself a pity party, but I refuse to let the pit control my life. I decline to make rash decisions on a really bad day. And I actively rebuff any temptation for a quick fix to my emotional pain. To do so would be to stunt my growth and become foolish, I'm sure.

Trust God

I'm choosing instead to sit in the pit and take God with me. I cry out to him, talk with him, and question him. And I listen . . . and sometimes, though not as often as I would like, he speaks. "Be still and know that I am God," he reminds. "I can be trusted with the things of this life that you will never have the privilege of understanding until heaven," he consoles. I know that is true. And so I rest in the pit. And so can you. The first steps to finding emotional readiness for dating are to rest in the pit you're in, trust God with what you don't understand, and look into the mirror he provides. Then and only then can you grow with his wisdom.

Explore Your Emotional History

An often hidden aspect of emotional readiness stems from our family of origin and relational history. It's one thing to ponder how your first love has impacted who you are now, but it's another to consider the relational patterns that persist throughout your life. Like threads that are woven into a fabric, relationship patterns create the narrative of our lives and heavily influence our thoughts, behaviors, emotional responses, and choices.

Cindy was bitter. "Men are pigs," she said. And then she connected the dots for me. Cindy's grandfather was a hard-working, happy-all-the-time drunk. As a young child she loved being around him because he was so jovial. As a young woman she realized how much his family despised him because, although he was responsible enough to provide for the family financially, his love affair with alcohol made him functionally absent from their lives. He was home all the time, but never there. Cindy's father, just like his father, left the family. When she was sixteen, her father left the home one day and never came back. "He had been in my life every day until then," she explained, "and then he was gone forever." Then came her first husband, who followed suit and left her for another woman when she was pregnant. For five years she lived as a single mom with no support. "Men are pigs; you can't trust them." Most recently she met Winston, fell in love, and married him within a year. Despite being warned by friends, it was only after she married him that she noticed that he catered to his ex-wife, who was demanding and controlling of his children. Believe it or not, Cindy never saw the relational pattern of irresponsible men in her life until I spelled it out for her. Neither did she understand her part in perpetuating the pattern by the men she chose, nor the blinders she put on while dating them.

You must—if you intend to ever have a relationship different from the ones you've had before—reflect on your relational history and ask the question *What does this tell me about me?*

This isn't intended to cast blame for all the bad things that have happened in your life, but to simply notice what the narrative of your life says about you.

- What types of relationships are you most familiar with (and, therefore, likely to repeat)?
- In hindsight, what are your blind spots about yourself or relationships?
- What roles do you and others typically play in your life?
- What vulnerabilities do you have?
- Based on the past, what beliefs do you have about men/women, husbands/wives, parents/stepparents, children/stepchildren?
- Knowing that previous emotional injuries lead us to look out for similar hurtful behavior from others, what wounds do you have on your heart and how would you know if you were hypersensitive to them, and therefore more likely to exaggerate the negativity of minor irritations?

These questions are crucial to finding emotional readiness for dating. Finding the right person who will love you just as you desire is not the answer to resolving the You issue. You must deal with you long before you try to get someone else to deal with you. If you are having difficulty with this, consider sitting down with a family therapist who will conduct a genogram with you. A genogram is a family map that helps someone explore their relationship history, spiritual legacy, and emotional well-being. It can be a very insightful process and help you to move out of unhealthy relationship ruts and cope with emotional bruises.

Timing Issues

I've got a hard truth for you. If it ain't over, it ain't over—and even if it's over, it ain't over. Let me explain.

Pam was positive that her boyfriend's marriage was over. Gary, who had been married for a total of nine years, had been separated for the last two and a half years. When Pam and Gary met, she was reluctant at first to date him, since his divorce was not final. Gary reassured her that his feelings for his soon-to-be ex-wife had ended long ago, and the only reason he was still married was because she was emotionally unstable and stubborn. She was contesting the divorce yet all the while living with a new boyfriend. "It's just her bitterness," he shared apologetically. "That's the only reason we aren't divorced. She shacked up with her boyfriend a few months ago, so she has obviously moved on—and as far as I'm concerned, it's over."

Something in Pam made her hesitant to date Gary, but his explanation and genuine interest in her lessened her defenses. Before long, Pam was dating Gary on a regular basis. But the marriage wasn't really over. About six months later, Gary's wife kicked out her boyfriend and had a change of heart. She let Gary know that she was interested in getting back together. Ironically, it was Pam who had wisdom enough to advise Gary to consider it. Pam's parents had divorced when she was a child, and she knew how hard it was to grow up with a stepparent. She urged him to explore the possibility of reconciliation even though it meant she and he would have to stop dating.

Pam and I processed the experience together. She learned that *almost over* is not the same as *over*. Rather than a clearly defined relationship environment, a not-yet ending offers ambiguity, which is really bad for starting something new. Pam also recognized:

- an ambiguous couple relationship is doubly confusing for kids.
- when a marriage isn't legally over, children, society, and the church define the new relationship as adulterous. That sets a poor moral example for children and invites them to emotionally boycott your relationship from the beginning.
- until the divorce was final, Gary couldn't fully put away his feelings for his wife. Even though they were bitter toward

each other, he could not be emotionally, psychologically, or spiritually released from her until their marriage ended and there was no possibility for reconciliation. And he couldn't know what he wanted in a relationship other than someone who would rescue him from his pit of pain.

Pam was only shooting herself in the foot (or should I say heart?) by dating him. It ain't over till it's over. Now here's part two: Even when it's over, it ain't over.

Divorce may be the end of love, but divorce also includes the persistence of attachment. In my first book, *The Smart Stepfamily,* I shared this key principle to understanding the ongoing relationship between ex-spouses: Divorce doesn't end family life, it only reorganizes it.

This truth has two aspects to it. First, couple interactional patterns that occur before a divorce usually continue after the divorce, as well. A man who catered to his ex-wife's ideas about parenting typically keeps catering well after they have divorced and set up two separate households. A woman who is critical and condescending toward her husband tends to be angry and picky well after their divorce. These patterns only change if one or both ex-spouses mature as individuals, accept how they negatively contributed to the end of the relationship, and choose to behave in different ways. The irony, of course, is that when exes are stuck in old interactional ruts, they keep their emotional attachments alive. This can hamper the development of new relationships. New love is much freer to mature when it is unencumbered by old emotional attachments.

A second aspect of this truth is that divorce doesn't end the job of parenting, it just reorganizes it. Two people who share a child never stop being in relationship with each other (we call them co-parents), and new partners must accept this. Even if their marriage is over, their parenting relationship isn't. In practical terms, this means that stepparents sometimes get vetoed out of decision making, have to deal with unfair financial arrangements, and have to confront the fear that ex-spouse parent-talk could easily slip into former spouse love-talk.

If you or the person you date cannot cope with the power-lessness this sometimes brings, the "always second, never first" nature of your relationship, or the related "you're not my mom/dad" stiff-arm from a stepchild, then you are in for a world of discouragement and distress and should back away from dating. I can't tell you how many newly married stepparents have said to me, "I don't know what I was thinking, but I just assumed that once we got married, his/her ex wouldn't interfere with our family. I thought it would just be us." Nothing could be further from reality. When kids are involved, marriage is a package deal. And the package includes exes and co-parenting in addition to the kids. If you can't marry the package, don't marry the person.

The larger point here is to pay attention to the timing of new relationships and not downplay the significance of ongoing attachments. Don't think you or a dating partner can skip adequate grieving and jump untouched and unscathed into a new relationship. Timing matters because it either contributes clarity and definition to the relationship, or it offers ambiguity and confusion; make sure it is the former.

So how long should someone wait after a death or divorce before dating again? I'm asked that question all the time by the media and single parents. I used to give them a definitive answer: Wait at least two years before dating. To be honest, I now consider that response inadequate and a bit arrogant. I thought I could give a one-size-fits-all response, but life, research, and experience has taught me that I can't. Timelines are misleading (they give a false sense of security) and deceiving (I know lots of people who aren't ready to date after five years!). No one can tell you how much time you need to mature or whether someone is ready to date. Now, having said that, I feel the need to offer this caution: In general, a quick turnaround is not conducive to wise relationship decision making. Rather, make time your friend. Use it to seek stability in your life, grow as a Christ-follower, and continually work toward a collaborative co-parenting relationship with your ex—and look for the same in whomever you date. People who rush into dating are usually running from something.

Gap Worries

Let me speak frankly to a vulnerability that weighs heavily on the hearts of many single parents. You care deeply for your children; that's why you want to fill any emotional and financial gaps they may have. For example, single moms who don't have the income potential they desire may feel great pressure to find a provider for the family. And parents who want their children to grow up in a home with both a mom and a dad may try to fill the gap with a man or woman willing to play the role. This gap worry is especially acute when a child openly asks for a dad or mom and the other biological parent is deceased or is MIA. Such gaps are undeniable. But replacement dating to give your child a two-parent home with a larger income is never a good idea.

Michelle has some gap worries. "Because I have a son, I feel strongly about getting married so that he will have a good, strong Christian male in his life so he can learn how to be a man and a godly leader. My son's father lives twelve hours away, so the only time he gets to spend with another male is when his grandparents keep him (about once every other month, which isn't much). I want my son to grow up in a two-parent home." Michelle's worries are understandable, but here's something she—and you—must comprehend. Even if Michelle marries, she is not giving her son a two-parent home. She would instead be giving her son a parent-stepparent home. They are not the same.

Yes, stepfamilies can be redemptive, loving, healthy environments for children. And yes, as I've written elsewhere, blended families have many rewards, such as providing children with positive marital role models, more stable economic conditions, and psychological healing from the negative impact of divorce.[1] But you can never fully restore the emotional process of a biological family; a parent-stepparent home does not equal a biological two-parent home. If it did, the outcome measures of child well-being would be similar for children of stepfamilies and biological homes. They aren't.

Findings from a national survey by the National Center for Health Statistics reveal considerable differences between children raised in nuclear families and those raised in single-parent families, blended, cohabiting, or extended families. Children in biological homes are generally healthier, have better access to health care, and are less likely to have definite or severe emotional or behavioral difficulties. Specifically, children in blended families do about as well as children in single-parent families on most outcome measures of well-being.[2] The point is this: Marrying someone just to fill the gaps in your child's life isn't wise.

Upon hearing this perspective, some single parents feel discouraged, as if I'm saying they would be wrong to date. That's not what I'm saying at all. Other single parents feel relieved when they hear this viewpoint because they realize there's no pressure to get married. That's exactly what I'm saying. Don't let guilt or worry be your motivation toward marriage. Marry someone, not as a replacement parent, but because you love them and believe they will help you raise your kids in the Lord. Until that person comes along, raising your children as a single parent is a viable option.

RELATIONAL ROADBLOCKS, BLINDNESS, AND BITTERNESS

Being blind to issues in a relationship is very different from being bitter over a previous one, but they have a similar function: neither brings wisdom or discernment about a new relationship. Relationship roadblocks just stop you in your tracks.

Ginny was blind. "Before we married, my husband and I did not seek out education on being a blended family because we didn't realize that it would be hard. Now, seven years into our marriage, I wish that we would have."

Kari also had a blind spot—about her child. She called Smart Stepfamilies after hearing me on a radio interview. Kari's daughter Bonnie (age twenty-five) fully resented her mother's remarriage three years after her father died in a car accident. Kari thought she had waited long enough but now realizes she missed a big yellow flag. "My daughter never talked about her dad's death. My son did, but Bonnie never wanted to talk about it. Now I'm three years in and I'm about to give up on having a blended family."

Courtney had a bruise on her heart from a previous relationship that blocked her from moving forward. "I love reading your e-magazine. I'm recently divorced and not nearly ready for another marriage for some time, but I do want to educate myself, because that may happen at some point. I was married for four years and have two children. My ghost is trust. My ex-husband consistently lied to me and had an affair. I find it very difficult to trust right now. I want to trust and fall in love again, but I'm very cautious and taking my time." Notice that Courtney is not blind to her roadblock trust issue—that is a huge plus. Yet she still has to deal with it.

And finally, do you remember Cindy, who decided after being abandoned by her grandfather, father, and first husband that "all men are pigs"? She was bitter, blind, and blocked. But can you blame her? Look, there is no condemnation for those who are hurt and, therefore, hesitant to move into another relationship, but you can't stay there. Whether you are going to date or not, dealing with your pain is critical to finding healthy living, becoming an effective parent, and perhaps, finding readiness for a new relationship. Recognize and deal with your stuff. Listen to trusted friends who can see into your blind spots. And then have the courage to face what you find.

I'll never forget the following post to SmartStepfamilies.com, because the unnamed writer impressed me with her courage. See if you agree.

> *My fiancé and I attended your conference in Dallas a year ago. We had been together almost a year and thought we had the perfect union and that it was time to blend our kids. After attending such an informative and discussion-provoking conference, we both knew that we weren't ready for marriage. Our kids weren't ready, either. We were in love with being in love and weren't thinking of how this would affect our kids. Your conference opened our eyes to how our kids' lives would be affected, and I am forever grateful. We broke off our engagement shortly thereafter and are both thankful that we had such wise counsel and good tools to help us in our decision-making process. As much as it hurt to say good-bye to each other, we do have the peace to know that it was the right decision.*
>
> *I would encourage anyone who is thinking of getting married and blending their children to RUN to this conference and also read your books NOW. You will walk away either knowing that you are really ready for this huge commitment, or that you have more to work on. Thank you so much for helping us. God's best to you!*
>
> *—Forever Grateful in Texas*

Now this is a couple with objectivity to see their bitterness, roadblocks, and blind spots when pointed out and the courage to face them head on. Preserving their fantasy relationship was not their priority; considering what was best for their children, families, and future was. Doing so steered them toward dissolving the relationship (that certainly won't always be the end result for others) and they embraced it. Likewise, if you find that you or the person you're dating is not emotionally ready for dating, I pray that you can bow out with courage and grace.

Discussion Questions

1. How does the recommendation that you stop worrying about whether you're ready to date and stop trying to discern whether the kids are ready for you to date, and instead "try it and see what happens" help take the pressure off? How does it inform what you should expect of yourself in dating?

2. Write out or share how you would know beyond a shadow of a doubt if you *weren't* ready to date.

3. How are you "relaxing in your aloneness"? How about the person you're dating?

4. List the relational patterns that persist throughout your life (family of origin and previous relationships). What themes rise to the surface, and how have they impacted your life and relationship choices so far? Consider these questions:

   • What types of relationships are you most familiar with (and therefore, likely to repeat)?

   • In hindsight, what are your blind spots about yourself or relationships?

   • What roles do you and others typically play in your life?

   • What vulnerabilities do you have?

   • Based on the past, what beliefs do you have about men/women, husbands/wives, parents/stepparents, children/stepchildren?

   • Knowing that previous emotional injuries lead us to look for similar hurtful behavior from others, what wounds do you have on your heart and how would you know if you were hypersensitive to experiencing them again?

5. What are the implications of this statement for you: If it ain't over, it ain't over—and even if it's over, it ain't over. ,

6. What gap worries (concerns that you believe only another adult can fill for your kids) have you had?

7. Review the roadblocks, blinders, and bitterness expressed by Ginny, Kari, Courtney, and Cindy. Can you see yourself in any of their descriptions?

Chapter 4

The Fear Factor: Preparing Yourself and the Kids for Dating

When I'm protecting me from you there can't be an us.

There's one more emotional readiness factor that must be considered, and it's so significant I've dedicated two chapters to the topic. Some people first encounter this factor even before they start dating, and others don't notice it till they are approaching marriage. But over twenty years of stepfamily training, research, and counseling has taught me that nearly every dating single experiences fear to some degree at some point—and so do the kids. If left unmanaged, fear in yourself, your partner, or the children has the ability—separate and apart from all the other stumbling blocks of blended families—to singlehandedly dismantle your relationship and paralyze your life.

After being tossed aside by her husband of sixteen years and the father of her two children, Lauren declared to friends in her divorce recovery group, "Never again will I be hurt like that." Her bitterness combined with the fear of being hurt again built twenty-foot walls of self-protection around her. And yet after many years of single living, to her surprise, Lauren found herself entertaining thoughts of romance. She wondered if she could love and trust again. But just when she'd begin to trust, fear would rush in. Even imagining being vulnerable made her heart tremble.

Stacy, on the other hand, had casually dated a few men. She found herself caught between hope and doubt, between the accelerator and the brake. Her children's reactions confused her, as well. One minute they were complimenting her date and the next complaining that she was going out again. "What does it all mean?" she asked. "It feels like walking through a minefield."

Lauren's and Stacy's fears had direct connections to having experienced divorce and being parents. For others the fear has more to do with their family of origin. Never-married Ming-hoa, a third-generation Asian-American, grew up with highly controlling traditional Chinese parents. While their high expectations did challenge him to do well in school and college, he never believed that he quite measured up. In short, Ming-hoa worried about pleasing others, and it came out in his dating relationships. Dating Jodie, a mother of two teenagers, had him sinking in anxiety. He not only worried about what Jodie thought of him, he worried about what her kids thought, too.

Essentially, fear is the emotion most apt to cause one or both partners to be guarded with their whole selves, cautious with their trust, calculating in determining how much they are willing to serve and sacrifice for the other, and careful not to step off the ledge of self-sufficiency. Fear is an excellent catalyst for self-preservation, but when I'm protecting me from you, there can't be an us. Fear prevents people from doing the things that love would have them do. It prevents them from choosing risk. Ironically, risk management behavior can lead to a self-fulfilling prophecy in which the self-protective person inadvertently contributes to the very thing they fear, that is, a distant or difficult relationship.

Kids of all ages have their own fears, too. They fear losing connection and time with their parent, they fear how one parent dating will impact the other parent, and they may fear losing their family identity, traditions, or inheritance. It's when kid fears intersect with adult fears that things really get complicated.

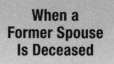

When a Former Spouse Is Deceased

Widows may fear the pain of another loss, but may also blindly assume a new marriage will be just as good as the previous one.

Hernando and Connie came for therapy just one month before their wedding. She had two teenagers from a previous relationship and he had two younger children. Because Connie had jumped into a relationship with Hernando fairly quickly, she had not processed her trust fears. But this fear surfaced rapidly once conflict between her son and fiancé increased.

One of Connie's teens, Samuel, was going through a period of rebellion and anger over his parents' divorce. She had hoped he and Hernando would connect, but Samuel wasn't open to Hernando. Instead he aligned himself closely with his father; this loyalty kept him closed to Hernando. The emotional disconnect between Hernando and Samuel escalated when Hernando confronted Samuel about how he was disrespecting Connie. Connie stepped in to manage the conflict, but as most "referee" parents discover, she alienated herself from both her fiancé and her son. Just one month before their marriage, everyone's fears were colliding, conflict was rising, and the couple was considering delaying the wedding.

Fear is hazardous to relationships. If you are going to date well, and ultimately have a successful marriage and family, dating must occur with an awareness of both adult and child fears. We'll examine adult fears in this chapter and kid fears in the next.

ADULT DATING FEARS

I fear parenting as a stepmom and having my kids parented by a stepdad.

Tammy, mom

I'm scared of my son being hurt and divorce happening all over again.

Jackson, dad

There are many different types of relational fears. Some of the most common are mentioned below. As you review them, ask yourself which may currently be at work in your life or dating relationship. Gauge the intensity of each fear on a scale of 1 to 10 (with 10 being the most intense and most menacing, 1 being just an occasional concern, and 5 being moderately troubling). Measuring and then addressing your fear factor is critical throughout every stage of dating. The lower the rating, the better, but be honest with your self-assessment.

As you consider each of the following, keep in mind this important insight: The more important the person and the more intimate the relationship (meaning transparent and connected), the more vulnerability, and therefore fear, increases. Just when you think it's safe to jump back into the deep end, fears sometimes swell. Many people don't register anything on their fear-o-meter until the word *marriage* gets thrown out, when they start thinking through the logistics of combining homes, children, possessions, and financial assets, or for some, when they actually get married. That's when things get real, fast. Don't be surprised by this; it's a natural outgrowth of a meaningful relationship. The upside of fear is that it testifies to the importance of the person. The reason you get anxious about the future is that you desire the other person in your life. And again, given what you have already been through (your loss story), leaning in to another person or family situation should produce some anxiety. Don't be taken aback by this—but don't deny it, either.

You see, what most people do when fear comes is to try and control relationship boundaries and expectations in order to mitigate their fear. For example, early on in the process, one dad didn't tell his kids he was dating. Surprisingly, he also didn't tell his dates that he had children. He justified it by saying things like, "What they don't know won't hurt them," and "Why make things complicated in the beginning in case things don't work out?" This need to control information is really about this dad's fears and ends up creating deception and mistrust.

Here's another example of how fear manifests itself. Lots of couples these days gravitate toward stayover and cohabiting relationships. These halfway house scenarios help people feel safe while still being in a serious relationship. But that's exactly the point. Stayover relationships—where each person maintains a personal residence but one of them stays over with the other on a fairly regular basis—and cohabitation are for many couples fear metaphors. The arrangement screams, "Since we're unwilling to jump with both feet into the deep end of life together, let's live together so we can maintain our options. That way you can have me and I can have you but neither of us really has to go all in—you know, just in case it goes bad." In seeking to control the risks inherent in a trusting relationship, these couples opt for an independent-togetherness arrangement.

The way through fear is not to sidestep it with a pseudo-promise that leaves the back door open. Rather, it is to acknowledge your fears, understand their origins and what they seek to protect you from, and then walk directly through them by choosing to risk. Love comes with risks; avoiding that truth gives in to fear.

Losing Kid Connection

In chapter 1 I mentioned an important truth that single parents must understand. The process of becoming a couple and ultimately placing significant priority on the couple relationship requires a shift of your energy and time away from your kids and to your spouse. This nearly always creates a competition of attachment and a loss of excessive closeness with your children. Death or divorce throws you into a survival closeness with your children that cannot be sustained when a marriage enters the picture. Something has to change—and kids feel the loss of connection. Single parent Jenny feared this very thing. "My biggest fear is that I will lose the quality time and relationship I have with my kids." Losing some connection is to be expected; the real question is how much will you lose.

One blind spot for single parents is assuming this dynamic will not apply to them because they have enough love for everyone. Of course you have enough love, but you don't have unlimited energy and you can't be in two places at once. Unless your children are toddlers, expect them to feel displaced and be irritated, jealous, or angry about it. One fourteen-year-old boy told me three years into his mom's remarriage, "I used to be best friends with Mom. But I got pushed back to fifth place when she met Benny."

In chapter 1, I introduced you to Rachel, a twenty-two-year-old student who feels the contrast in her mom's investment in her boyfriend versus her. "Sometimes I get frustrated that she will tell me she's 'too busy to talk—can it wait?' when I know that she talks to him every morning and evening. Pushing me out of her schedule when she has multiple slots can be frustrating, but she doesn't see it that way. I also get frustrated when she spends lots of money to see him yet complains about finances. When he is available she clears her schedule; when I come back from school, her work schedule stays the same and she often takes phone calls during our time together. She would never do that with him."

Here's the tough part. Rachel's mother isn't necessarily doing anything wrong. She is just giving part of her time and affections to someone other than her daughter. For Mom, this is a good thing. For Rachel, it's another loss—a change she didn't want or ask for. Those who are dating a single parent may find this dynamic bewildering or troubling. It's hard to imagine how much pain the children have already experienced in life and, therefore, why your presence can cause more unhappiness in the child. Resist the temptation to complain to your dating partner that their kids are out of line. Instead, listen with compassion and try to have grace for how difficult this is for them.

If as a single parent you can't face the fear that dating will likely create in your children—and your resulting guilt—don't date. If you can, pair moving forward with compassion toward the kids because, again, life seems a little out of tune with their needs and family agenda. Most important, stay as active in their lives and as emotionally affirming as you can; they need to see that they really haven't lost you.

How strong is this fear in your life? Rate 1 to 10.

Causing Kid Pain

A loss of relationship connection certainly causes some kids pain. But pain can come about in other ways, as well. Kyle worries that "if I get serious with someone and things don't work out, the kids will have formed an attachment to that person and be hurt by the loss and/or become desensitized to later relationships." This is a legitimate concern. Very young children can sometimes bond with a parent's dating partner faster than the parent can, so be sure not to prematurely expose children to a dating partner (see the next chapter for guidelines on introducing kids to dating partners).

Angela has already had one bad dating relationship and doesn't want her daughter to grow increasingly bitter about men and dating. She also doesn't want to bring a man into the house who will expose her daughter to unhealthy behaviors or actions, so she is vigilant to only date men who have a proven record of spiritual integrity.

In addition, Angela is fearful of a marriage where her daughter is not fully accepted. Like most fears, this one has some truth to it and some exaggerated concern. It's true, for example, that stepparents do feel differently about stepchildren than they do their biological children. That's not to say that they don't love them, but that they love them more by choice than by a natural connection, especially during the early seasons of the blended family. If a biological parent's standard for the stepparent is that they love stepchildren and biological children the same, everyone will be discouraged; that standard just isn't realistic. But how much less are you willing to accept?

One final significant fear is inadvertently exposing your children to an emotional or sexual predator. No one purposefully chooses to do so, but it happens. There are warning signs to look for: someone who refuses to take responsibility and continually blames others for their failures, has a sense of entitlement and uses people for their own benefit, lacks empathy for the pain of others, struggles with intimate relationships, has a history of abuse or a troubled childhood, or engages in deviant sexual behavior and abuses pornography.[1] But even with that list in mind, it's possible to be duped given that predators are excellent manipulators. You must be aware of this fear (and the signs of an abuser) and find balance in how cautious you will be.

How strong is this fear in your life? Rate 1 to 10.

Not Blending

Another common fear I hear repeated from singles is the fear that the family won't blend. What if holiday traditions can't be united? What if differing parenting styles can't be brought in line or if spending habits and financial assets bring disagreement and possessiveness? Cathy shared, "I fear having my best intentions misunderstood by my stepchildren or that some of them may never completely accept me—that, plus simultaneously watching my kids experiencing another loss (of me) while I try to connect with my stepkids."

In the beginning, blended families are not blended. In fact, they are a collection of two families living under the same roof, trying to integrate their lives. It is important that you recognize that some family members may not fully integrate themselves. Adult stepchildren, for example, or a teenager who has primary residence at the other home doesn't get much integration time with the new family and, therefore, may not connect into the new family identity. You must consider this a possibility as you date and count the cost should you marry.

This is a very real fear for singles without children dating single parents. Think about it: If you marry someone with four kids, and for whatever reason you aren't accepted, it could be five against one really fast. In response to this fear, I've watched some singles subtly try during dating to distance their dating partner from their children. That is a big mistake. Never try to distance or, for that matter, substantially alter the bond between a parent and their children because it will only rebound against you. Don't try to manipulate the relationship of others to make space for you. If you can't deal with the ambiguity while finding your fit with them, step back.

How strong is this fear in your life? Rate 1 to 10.

Choosing Poorly

"Personally, I fear repeating the same mistake," said Carl. "I pray that God helps me find the best woman for me and that I don't jump into a bad situation. I worry that she will be completely different after a year." Chandra's biggest fear is "picking the wrong man again, or jumping in too soon and not getting the best that God wants for me." Falling in love makes everyone believe they have chosen wisely, but life sometimes reveals that you chose poorly.

In a way, that's not completely fair. I believe that some people choose a mature, godly mate, but life and circumstances bring out the worst in them. It's not like finding the right person will always result in the best behavior from them, or even the best family with you. Don't get me wrong, I want you to pay attention and pick well (chapter 7 will reveal some caution lights to heed and stoplights not to run), but be realistic: We all have faults. Ask yourself if you are willing to love an imperfect person. Are you willing to allow God to stretch you in order to mature your relationship with someone who is at times inadequate and flawed? One of the reasons God gives our spouses failings is so he can grow us.

How strong is this fear in your life? Rate 1 to 10.

Ex-Spouse Fear

Ex-spouses can wreak lots of havoc on remarriage relationships. From causing financial stress when they won't pay their share of child medical bills to overt flirtations and sexual propositions, ex-spouses carry leverage to invade your relationships. Diane's anxiety would rise every time she even thought about dating because of her ex-husband's emotional instability. He was possessive and controlling during their marriage, and she feared that if she brought another man into her life and the lives of their children he would escalate his bad behavior.

In Jack's dating relationship it was only after two years that he admitted how much the ex-spouse factor bothered him. "Both the lady I have been dating and I have been divorced for over ten years. I have four young adult children and she has two. The reason we haven't married yet is because of her relationship with her ex-husband. They still speak two to four times a week—and most of it is unnecessary. Should I just give up?"

Here's the bind when it comes to ex-spouses: Because they share children, they should and must communicate on a regular basis. Interaction is unavoidable, but that communication should be restricted to parental dialogue, not personal conversation (see my book *The Smart Stepfamily* for a full discussion of boundaries with ex-spouses). Ex-spouses who regularly cross the line toward the personal create a threat to new romantic attachments. If the appropriate boundaries cannot be maintained, something has to give. In other words, my answer to Jack's question, "Should I give up?" is this: If others confirm to you that her connection with her ex is too close, express your concerns. If she continues to ignore your need for firmer boundaries, then yes, give up and move on.

How strong is this fear in your life? Rate 1 to 10.

Fearing Spiritual Judgment

For many Christians, remarriage brings spiritual judgment from their church or Christian brothers and sisters. Different understandings of what constitutes an unscriptural marriage can polarize friends and family members. Other times, the spiritual fear comes from within. Jamie wrote to me asking, "What if you are the one causing the spiritual pain? My husband and I had an affair that ended our first marriages. I wish so badly that I could go back in time. I always have to live with the fact that I am the other woman who caused pain to so many. I dare not ask God to bless our marriage. Adultery and divorce are devastating; no wonder God hates divorce. He does not want his children suffering the consequences, but my husband and I live them every day."

If you are in Christ, the sin of the past will be forgiven. But even if Jamie and her husband can embrace God's radical grace, they will have to live with some very real consequences of their sin. None of us can change the past, but we can live faithfully (not perfectly!) beginning today. If you're finding it difficult to accept God's forgiveness, seek wise counsel from a Christian therapist or pastor.

How strong is this fear in your life? Rate 1 to 10.

CHASING AWAY THE GHOSTS

Now that you're more aware of your fears and the ghosts that haunt you, what do you do about them? Trusting that your ratings for the fears mentioned above are accurate, anything that is a 5 or greater needs attention. These ghosts will creep into your heart and relationship at some point and you need to chase them away. But how?

Before addressing that, let me say something counterintuitive; you are under no moral obligation to walk through your fears. I know that sounds strange, but as a single person, you don't have to overcome your fears. If you were already married and came asking how to overcome them, my response to you would be different: "Okay. You've made a covenant before God that is going to require you to walk through your fears and do what love demands. Let's get to work." But single people don't have that moral obligation. Being cautious might mean you miss out on a relationship, but you certainly are free to make that choice. As long as your dating relationship is honest, rooted in spiritual integrity, and sexually pure, you don't have to walk through your fears. If, however, you desire to work through them, consider these key steps.

First, lay before the Lord your desire to be free of the fears that limit your ability to love selflessly. Continually invite him to help identify what triggers your fear and how it makes you react. This self-awareness is crucial to changing your response set. Essentially, you must become familiar with how fear impacts you and what your typical reaction is. Once you identify it, I suggest you write this down so it becomes tangible and real to you. You might even run it by a trusted friend or counselor who can give outside perspective on that part of you. Together, you'll get a much more complete picture of the measure of your fear and how it debilitates you.

Then, ask yourself these critical questions: If I didn't have any fears, if I didn't have any emotional bruises on my heart from the past and I wasn't afraid to risk being hurt again, how would I respond in this situation? What would love have me do in this situation? What would I do if I didn't have anything to lose? This, too, should be something you share with a trusted friend so they can help you shape this "free to love" scenario. Then, begin to push through your fear and take the risks love would have you take. Ralph Waldo Emerson once said, "Do the thing you fear and the death of fear is certain." There's profound wisdom in that. Ask God for strength and trust him to see you through.

After taking a good long look at her fears, Evelyn realized she found comfort in emotional and financial independence. Throughout her life she has dealt with strong, opinionated men. Her father was a military man with rigid black-and-white rules for her life. One of her boyfriends in high school controlled her time and friendships while they were dating, and her first husband was a high-powered attorney who expected their marriage and family life to center around his schedule and professional goals. Divorced now for nine years, Evelyn had come to find comfort in her independence and feared trusting herself and her kids to another man. "I am accustomed to being able to manage my own time and resources," she said. "I like being able to make decisions without having to consult another person."

Evelyn wrote down her fears as she identified them. She feared being trapped in a relationship, gravitating toward men who are abusive or controlling, finding herself in a bad marriage, having to parent small children again, having to share her finances with someone and their children, having her children not like someone she does like, and trusting and being hurt again. Then Evelyn noticed how each fear impacted her emotionally and what actions she typically undertook to prevent the fears from becoming reality. For example, she noticed that when she went on first dates, she asked lots of probing questions about the man's past;

her aim was to identify any markers of untrustworthiness as quickly as possible. Her guard was up, and she let it be known she didn't need anyone. Unfortunately, this callousness made her unattractive to the men she dated, who stopped pursuing her fairly quickly.

Of course, asking questions about someone's past is part of getting to know them. But looking for negativity (and perhaps inserting negativity when it wasn't there) to justify withholding herself was the problem for Evelyn. That's what she decided to change. Walking through that fear meant calming her anxiety while on first dates and becoming more of a listener and less of an investigative reporter looking for dirt. She told herself that taking things slowly was okay, as was lowering her emotional wall (a little wall was okay).

Similarly, Evelyn created a list of initial growth steps regarding each of her fears; together they helped her slowly move through her fear.

Now, let me jump around the other side of change for a moment. Balance your risk with appropriate boundaries. Some people have distorted ideas of ghost-free living and become easy targets for manipulative people. Loving with your whole heart doesn't mean living without boundaries. Instead it frees you to live out of your God-given worth and identity in Christ in the loving service of another. Self-respect based on what God has done (and is doing) in you is the source of your ability to give to another—and that giving will never belittle your identity in Christ.

For many people there is quite a contrast between who they are when paralyzed by fear and who they will be when it no longer has a hold. The journey into and through fear will be anxiety producing, but no pain, no gain.

Incidentally, going through this process will help you help your children with their fears.

Discussion Questions

1. React to this statement: Fear is an excellent catalyst for self-preservation, but when I'm protecting me from you, there can't be an us, because fear prevents people from doing the things that love would have them do. It prevents them from choosing risk, which leads to a self-fulfilling prophecy.

2. Work through the list of Adult Dating Fears and rate them on a scale of 1 to 10. Share why you rated each as you did.

   - Losing kid connection
   - Causing kid pain
   - Not blending
   - Choosing poorly
   - Ex-spouse fear
   - Fearing spiritual judgment

3. In addition to the fear examples provided in this chapter, what fears have you seen in yourself or others?

4. Given the evidence that cohabitation is detrimental to relationships, why does it remain so popular in our culture?

5. React to this statement: Stayover relationships and cohabitation are for many couples fear metaphors. The arrangement screams, "Since we're unwilling to jump with both feet into the deep end of life together, let's live together so we can maintain our options. That way you can have me and I can have you but neither of us really has to go all in."

6. React to this statement: As a single person, you are under no moral obligation to walk through your fears.

7. Consider these steps to chasing away the ghosts:

   - Lay before the Lord your desire to be free of the fears that limit your ability to love selflessly. Continually invite him to help identify what triggers your fear and how it makes you react. This self-awareness is crucial to changing your response set.

- Write down your fears so they are tangible and real to you. You might even run it by a trusted friend or counselor who can give outside perspective on that part of you.

- Ask yourself these critical questions: If I didn't have any fears, if I didn't have any emotional bruises on my heart from the past and I wasn't afraid to risk being hurt again, how would I respond in this situation? What would love have me do in this situation? What would I do if I didn't have anything to lose?

- Then, take the risk of loving in these ways. Risk is the only way to confirm or disprove your fears.

Chapter 5

Kid Fears and Dating Considerations

My son, Mason, is happy to have Kenny in our lives and looks forward to us getting married. He wants us to get engaged.

Mandy, single mom

I'm not comfortable being with Mom and her date; I don't even like seeing her with someone else. Dad's only been dead a year and already she's serious.

Britney, age 23

Don't date people your kids don't like.

Katie, age 14

Adults aren't the only ones with fears. Kids of all ages, young and adult, have them, too. Doug had been raising his thirteen-year-old daughter by himself for two years. Before then, Doug, his wife, and their daughter, Danielle, had a close family. They did everything together and seemed to be very happy with life. Then without warning, after seventeen years of marriage, Doug's wife announced that she was having an affair with her personal trainer and she left. And I mean, she *left*. She had been a highly engaged mother and wife, but when she walked out she never looked back. Doug never had a chance to win back his wife, and Danielle was completely abandoned by her mother. Doug and Danielle went into complete shock together and were forced into survival—together.

Two years later Doug lined up his first date. Needless to say, Danielle became very anxious. She and her mother had been enmeshed the first eleven years of her life, and still Mom left. Now she and her father were very close and had been surviving tragedy together, but life had already taught her not to trust closeness. She was no longer naïve to what could happen.

Before he left, Doug was able to reassure his daughter that this was just a first date and didn't really mean much to him. Still she remained anxious. During the date he received two phone calls, one voice mail, and three text messages. One text read, "I know you don't want to talk to me anymore, but I want to tell you something—have fun without me because I'm all by myself now."

Why did Danielle toss a guilt grenade at her father? Why before his second date with the same woman did this even-tempered teenager escalate to verbal criticism and provoking his anger by hitting him with her pillow and jabbing him with a fork?

KID REACTIONS

Some children are excited for a parent to begin dating, others go into a jealous rage, but nearly all kids are concerned to some degree. If a child's parents are divorced, dating signifies another nail in the coffin of reconciliation. If a parent is widowed, a move into dating could make a child wonder if their deceased parent is being forgotten or didn't mean as much to the widowed parent as they once thought. These and other troubling thoughts can occur at the very same time that a child expresses excitement that their parent is "getting out there" and doing something for themselves.

"I don't get it," one parent said to me. "My kids pushed me to date before I was even thinking about it—and once I did, they did a one-eighty on me and whined and complained. What's the deal?" Yeah, kid reactions can be confusing. The reason they do this is that they are confused, too. One side of them wants to see you smile again; another side of them is frightened by how life will change if someone new joins the family. But why? What causes the fears?

Essentially the same dynamic that causes adults to fear vulnerability and being hurt again causes kid fears—loss. Your children have lost contact with extended family members and a parent (after divorce, being with you means not being with the other, and death means losing contact permanently). They have lost control over their lives—they didn't choose the divorce, the move to a new residence and school, loss of friends, change of household income, etc. Even your decision to date is another change they may not have wished for. And they have lost predictability about the future. They, like you, have a before-and-after story that has forever changed their outlook on life. When recounting their loss story, children will tell you the unfortunate lessons they learned: People you trust can't be counted on to be trustworthy; life is fragile—one minute you're feeling safe and the next your world falls apart; sometimes parents say they love you and then they can't be reached; chaos and change means no one listens and you just have to figure things out on your own.

Each loss creates the fear of more loss, which in turn creates a sensitivity to anything that resembles loss, especially losses that involve parents and family members. Family attachments are highly prized by children under normal circumstances, but after loss, they are golden. When a parent dates, kids feel the shift in direction away from them and the family; this ignites their fear of more loss.

But in my view, what is more detrimental than the fear itself is when adults minimize or ignore the child's concern. That just substantiates the fear that they again are being left behind. When a parent repeatedly dismisses the child, the child's fear of being unimportant and on their own is confirmed. On the other hand, a wise single parent pays attention to kid fears before dating, and once dating, a wise couple gives consideration to the pace of their relationship and the needs of the children. It's not that kid fears should dictate whether you date, but there is a balance to be sought. Dating successfully involves attending to the child's fears by listening and acknowledging the legitimacy of their fears, and reassuring them of your continued dedication and presence in their lives. This reassurance must come in the form of both words of affirmation and time spent together. If they are ever to embrace a new spouse in your life or stepsiblings, they must come to believe that doing so is not the equivalent of self-sabotage.

Samuel approached me at a conference. "I'm dating a woman with two children," he said. "My two girls, ages twelve and ten, are jealous of her kids. They don't like me spending time with them, and my girls tell me negative things about them so I won't want to be close to them. It really bothers me." I explained to Samuel that his children were feeling displaced—and that this was predictable. Don't panic, I encouraged, just be sure to balance your time with your girlfriend, her kids, and yours—and repeatedly reinforce to your girls how much you love and are committed to them, because this fear may not go away quickly.

PREPARING THE KIDS: DO'S AND DON'TS

David and Donna arranged a meeting with me to discuss the next steps of their dating relationship. When I think of wise dating, I often think of their circumstances and how many good lessons others can learn from their story.

After twenty-eight years of marriage, Donna was widowed when her husband died of cancer. They enjoyed a full life together and had three children. When I met Donna, the oldest, Angela, was twenty-seven and married; the middle, Kaitlin, was twenty-one and in college; and the youngest, Darrell, was just finishing high school. The loss of their father had dealt the children a mighty blow. I struggle when trying to put words on the significance of loss to people—children in particular. Remember the before-and-after discussion of loss in chapter 2? Everything changes after divorce or the death of a loved one, and life becomes about survival and finding a new—and unwanted—normal. Angela, Kaitlin, and Darrell were trying to do just that when only a year later Mom met and started dating David.

Married for thirty-five years, David and his first wife divorced. They had two children: Jalynn, age thirty, and Matt, age twenty-six. A long process of disaffection preceded the divorce such that when it ended, David quickly began dating. Just a few months after the divorce became final, David met Donna.

Now in their mid-fifties, the couple dated about ten months before contacting me for guidance. Their children, of course, knew by then that they were dating, but none of them knew how serious things were. The couple was considering engagement, but Donna was worried about two of her kids and how they would react. David's children seemed to be fine with Donna, and Donna's youngest, Darrell, kind of liked David. They had a lot in common and connected pretty quickly. But Donna's two daughters were expressing a lot of fear about David. Because they were out of the house, they really didn't have much exposure to David, but it was more than that. They just weren't ready for Mom to be dating at all.

In our first conversation, David wanted to force the issue. "What if Donna and I just got engaged? Wouldn't that force the kids to grieve their dad a little more and get used to the idea of us being together?" I quickly recognized his strong desire to be with Donna, and acknowledged it.

But then I pointed out how that strong desire was blinding him to the significance of Angela's and Kaitlin's feelings. "It will likely do just the opposite," I said. "You can't rush grief or demand attachment. The girls would probably turn away from you and fear your relationship with their mother if you did that. I don't recommend it. Instead, stop trying to rush their acceptance; time is your friend. Let's be strategic from this point forward, but you must be patient with the process and respect the fears of the kids. Hopefully with time they will soften and begin to let you in, but only they can decide if and when they are ready for that."

I then shared the following principles with David and Donna and coached them as they moved forward. They both showed much courage and wisdom in implementing these ideas. After six months, progress had been made, but they still weren't where they had hoped to be.

Monitor the Two Rockets, Two Trajectories

I explained to David and Donna that their relationship was like a launched rocket and the kid dynamic was a totally separate rocket, and each had to be monitored and managed independently of the other. And if that wasn't enough, I went on to explain that the two rockets had launched at different times, at different speeds, and were heading on different trajectories. Their couple rocket managed liftoff many months before the kids knew anything about it and was headed at top speed toward Passion Planet. It was only then that all five of the kids' rockets took off, each at their own speed and trajectory (determined by the child). Three of the kid rockets seemed to be keeping pace with David and Donna's rocket, but for some reason

Angela's and Kaitlin's rockets were traveling at a very slow rate of speed and were headed toward Maybe Moon. Maybe they would make room for David in their hearts, and maybe they wouldn't. Maybe they would feel safe with the changes to their family, and maybe they wouldn't. Finally, I pointed out an important but not so obvious reality to David and Donna: Each of your children is pilot of their own rocket—not you. You can't will them into flying faster or going your direction. Because they are Donna's kids, she will carry more anxiety about this; David will probably carry more frustration. Mom should stay connected and open to the ongoing dialogue with each as she monitors and manages this dynamic in the dating relationship. David should stay focused on developing a relationship with the girls as he has opportunity. At times it won't feel like much, I explained, but that is how you fly.

> ### If You Don't Have Kids
>
> Dating a single parent can get frustrating if you feel the speed of your couple rocket is being slowed by the speed and trajectory of the kids' rockets. You are used to living life unencumbered; don't think you can force your timeline on the kids or the person you are dating.

Reassure Biological Family Connections

As I said earlier, competing attachments are inevitable when a parent starts dating. So the first course of action for the single parent is to not force your dating partner on the kids or expect them to embrace the relationship (what most people try to do). Rather, the best first thing is for the biological parent to reassure their children of their continued presence, love, and commitment. Kids of every age need to know they can be sure of you. Parents often take this for granted; children, however, do not. If accepting your dating partner feels like losing you, your partner won't stand a chance. Reassure with your words and by balancing time alone with them and time alone with your dating partner.

Engage in "What If?" Conversations

I wish that all single parents would start a "What if?" dialogue with their children long before they begin dating. "What if I started dating, how would you feel?" This question is both assessment and intervention. The child's response helps you assess their openness to the idea of you dating (and you'll get a much more honest response if you aren't yet dating), and the discussion will prime their expectations and begin to get them prepared for it to happen someday. Other "What if?" questions, such as "What if I introduced you to someone—how would you feel? What if he had kids of his own? What if I got remarried someday?" softly introduce the potential realities and give you more information about your kids and their emotions.

> ### Kid Pace
>
> Remember the cardinal rule: Let the children set the pace for their developing relationship with your dating partner. If they are open and engaged, let them be. If they keep their distance, don't immediately demand that they open their hearts. Give them time to decide for themselves.

Unfortunately, like a lot of parents, Donna had not begun an ongoing "What if?" dialogue with her girls before dating David. It was time to start. I coached her to engage them individually and make listening her only agenda. It is tempting for parents to open this dialogue in order to push an acceptance agenda on the child. Kids see through this quickly and shut down, especially teenagers. Any hurt or anger that results closes the discussion and sabotages the parent's attempt to connect to the child's heart. If you listen, your child feels reassured of you; if you push an agenda, you increase the anxiety between you and diminish your influence.

If you have older teenagers or adult children, give *soft* invitations for them to join you and your partner. Hard, high-demand invitations dictate: "Come over for dinner tonight. I want you to get to know her." Soft invitations leave control with the child: "She will be having dinner with me Friday night. You are welcome to join us." Again, you don't want to sound like you're telling your adolescent or adult children to like your dating friend. Instead, show respect for their rocket speed and trajectory.

Acknowledge and Label Child Fears

Donna resisted trying to push an agenda on her girls when she engaged them in a few "What if?" conversations—and she learned some things she didn't want to hear. Her married, twenty-seven-year-old daughter, Angela, opened up. Angela knew this type of conversation might come up someday, and she dreaded it. She was aware that her mom was dating and admitted it confused her. "I'm just beginning to adjust to Dad being gone and thinking of you as a single mom, let alone you dating. I really don't know much about David, but it's not about him—I'm confused about you dating at all. I really don't know when I'll be ready for you to date." Her younger daughter, Kaitlin, was more direct. "Don't bring him to lunch when you come to see me. I'll decide when I want to be with the two of you." Trying to talk them out of these feelings may be tempting at this point. But when you start arguing with your child's feelings you have stopped trying to connect to their heart and have switched to the agenda of pushing them toward your partner.

Children of all ages, young to old, benefit when a parent says, "I can see that the idea of my dating scares you. You are missing Mom/our family/etc. and probably don't want any more changes to our family. I get it. I appreciate your being honest with me." Use phrases like "this scares you," "you're afraid that our family won't be the same," or "you don't want to have to change schools or leave your friends." This type of response validates the child's fears. It also shows them their feelings are important to you, keeps the communication door open, and helps children put labels on their own emotions (which is very important for young children especially).

Plus, it does one more important thing: It shows that you aren't afraid of or offended by their fears. Children are notorious for hiding their emotions because they don't want to hurt their parent's feelings. If you act fragile, they will treat you as fragile and hide from you. That discourages them from openly communicating with you and adds to a child's sense of isolation and loneliness—and makes welcoming your dating partner less likely. Show them you aren't fragile and can handle their emotions.

Don't Add Anxiety by Pushing an Acceptance Agenda

Donna connected with her girls on a regular basis. She called Angela (who lived out of town) to visit and had lunch with Kaitlin when they could. She wisely continued engaging her daughters in these one-on-one activities. At one point she asked me if she should mention David or bring up the "What if?" discussion fairly often. I basically told her no. Let most of your time together be mother-daughter time. To bring up David frequently is to have an acceptance agenda, and your daughters will feel pressure immediately. Don't constantly invade your time with an agenda; if you do, soon they will shy away from time with you, which only adds to a sense of isolation and loss—and fear.

> ### Part-time Kids
>
> Finding time for "What if?" conversations and processing fears with children who live with you part time can be challenging. Plus, they may withhold their feelings since they get little time with you. Take advantage of the time you do have to make this happen.

If they bring it up, fine, engage the conversation. Otherwise, save your David and "What if?" talk for purposeful occasions.

Honor Special Family Days With Family Members Only

At one point Donna and her children were getting together to acknowledge a special family day in honor of her deceased husband. Because everyone was going to be in town at the same time, she wondered if they couldn't carve out a little time for David to spend with the entire family. I suggested that doing so would run the risk of appearing opportunistic and would take the family's focus off their grief, something that very much needed its own space. Both she and David agreed not to muddy the waters and let the moment appropriately be about the children and their father.

Stay Patient

Have you noticed how much time this is taking? Walking out these principles could take weeks or months. Remember how eager David was in the beginning to get engaged and pull the kids into acceptance? In case you've forgotten, I'll say it again: It's one thing to become a couple, but becoming a family is a totally different process. Wise adults patiently let time be their friend as coupleness and familyness develop.

As I was writing this section, I decided to check in on Donna and David. Six months after our last conversation, Donna reported that Kaitlin, the child who had once said, "Leave it to me to decide when I'm ready to be with both of you," had invited David and her mom to join her at a concert. Donna noted that she had really poured herself into Kaitlin during the preceding six months and thought that strong connection had helped Kaitlin open up a little. I agreed.

Angela had also softened some and initiated a social occasion with both Mom and David. Donna was anticipating the dinner when we talked and was hopeful it would help David and Angela connect. "I'm sure it will," I replied. "But just remember that rocket is still pointed toward Maybe Moon. It will help, but remember to relax your expectations or everyone will feel pressure. That is how you get off course." Overall, Donna was feeling encouraged even though the kids were far from on board.

And what of David, you wonder? He was still practicing patience. Earlier I mentioned that biological parents often describe themselves more as anxious about how their children are responding to their dating partner, while the dating partner can feel frustrated with how slowly things seem to be progressing with the children. David was certainly feeling frustrated but kept reminding himself to love them with patience. He wrote me an email saying, "I have to confess that I teared up a little after I hung up the phone from our conversation today. You're right; it has been very hard to be patient as I've been systematically excluded by Donna's daughters from every gathering of her family for holidays and special events."

Common Kid Reactions

- The presence of a dating partner elicits sadness and a stiff-arm response.
- Kids are cordial and even encouraging of the relationship until it becomes serious.
- Often there are hot/cold responses throughout the relationship.
- Some kids can't wait to have a stepparent and siblings to play with.

He went on to share situations in which the girls' hesitation kept him from being part of some family activities. "It's hard to sit at home alone when you want to be with the one you love and you know that she is enjoying a good time at an extended-family gathering." At the same time, David was compassionate for the bind Donna felt between him and her girls. He knew being patient was what was required of him, but still it was frustrating. Perhaps the upcoming get-togethers initiated by the girls would make it all worth it, he thought.

That's when I predicted something. "Yes, time with her children will help them get to know you and see the reality of your relationship. Just remember that as your relationship deepens and gets more serious, a new wave of fear can occur in kids. For example, they may come to generally like you, but that doesn't necessarily mean they'll be happy with talk of marriage."

Sure enough, a few weeks later, David sent me an update. After a few get-togethers with David, Donna asked her kids the next "What if?" question: "What if David and I were to get engaged?" Here's his feedback. "Ron, you were right about their initial reaction when they first realized how serious our relationship is. All three of them ended up in tears when Donna asked them how they would feel about her getting serious with me. Donna sent me a text message immediately after that conversation saying she had gone into her bedroom to cry and didn't want to come out. But after her younger daughter went home, she had another talk with her older daughter that made her feel a little better. I went over that evening and shared with her your prediction—somehow that made us feel normal. The next day she was feeling better about it."

Remember: Different rockets with different trajectories is normal.

So now what do they do? Assuming the concern for their children's reactions remains generally low, they gently press forward with patient dialogue and sensitivity to the newfound fears. And Donna and David should adjust their expectations to assume that each new depth of their couple relationship will bring new anxieties and concerns in the children. Anticipating these realities will help them to be proactive and not taken off guard.

Should a Child's Fears Cause a Parent to Postpone Dating?

The answer to this question is not black and white; in other words, it depends. As I stated earlier, a parent who blindly dismisses a child's fear and pushes their concerns aside is engaging in self-sabotage and causing injury to a child's spirit. At the same time, a moderate level of fear is to be expected and can be soothed with time in many cases, so it may not necessitate the breaking up or slowing down of a dating relationship.

Go slow and move forward with much prayer and counsel from friends and family members you trust. Shelli listened to her friends and prayed about her situation. "I put off dating for a long time. My kids are okay with me dating now, but had I dated sooner, I think they would have had serious behavior problems, especially my middle daughter. Waiting until they got older has definitely been worth it, even if I didn't think so at the time."

I do think that some parents should consider not dating if their children are struggling emotionally or psychologically. Amy's sixteen-year-old son, Robert, was depressed and constantly isolating himself. No matter how hard Amy or the youth pastor tried, they couldn't get Robert to open up. He was hanging out with troubled students, and there were rumors of alcohol and marijuana abuse. Without question Amy needed to be available to her son during this season of his life, not distracted by a love interest.

But that's not fair, she needs a life, too, some may object. When has parenting ever been fair? This isn't about balancing your needs with theirs; this is about a lost child—your lost child—who needs your every effort in order to be found. How would it be fair for Amy to pursue her life while her child is miserable?

> **If You Don't Have Kids**
>
> Do your relationship a favor: Encourage the single parent you are dating to "go home" and be with their kids, without you, every once in a while. This has two benefits: (1) it helps lessen the fears of the children, and (2) it keeps perspective in your relationship.

MORE DO'S AND DON'TS

Through the years I've asked single parents and married couples in blended families to reflect on their best dating practices as they relate to children. Here is their collective wisdom.

Pace and Balance Your Dating

If you fall in love, don't abandon your kids by spending all of your free time with your newfound love. It's tempting, but doing so taps into your child's fears that they are losing you and gives the false impression to your dating partner that you are totally available to them. You're not. Don't lose your balance.

But this is more than just balancing time for the sake of your children. Monitor how your dating partner responds to this balanced approach—it will tell you something of their maturity and character. If they are easily offended that they are not the center of your universe, they will likely make for a whiney, jealous stepparent. Don't subject yourself and your kids to such a person; move on.

Introductions and Early Dating

Early on your kids may meet your date and be intrigued to learn a little about them, but try to make the first few dates primarily about the two of you. At first, reference your date as "a friend" or, if your kids are prepared, call them your "date." Casual introductions are fine when you start dating someone, but don't proactively put your kids and the person together until you are pretty sure there are real possibilities for a couple relationship. This is especially true for children under the age of five, who can bond to someone you are dating more quickly than you can. A quick attachment is a setup for pain when your casual relationship ends.

As your interest in the person grows, gradually become more intentional about finding time for your boy/girlfriend and kids to get together. Tread lightly at first and continue to monitor and process everyone's fear or concerns. Initially it can be helpful to both the children and a dating partner to know a little about the other before they spend time together. Share with each the interests they have in common and what you like about them. Then, plan a family outing so everyone can get to know one another. Be sure to let children know that you do not expect instant affection toward your dating partner, but you do, however, expect a basic respect for them as an adult.

If they ask questions (e.g., "Is he your boyfriend?" "Do you love him?"), be prepared to give your kids an honest but calculated response (that is, developmentally appropriate). For example, over time your response might shift from, "No, not a boyfriend. We're just beginning to get to know each other," to "Yes, I really like him and think of him as my boyfriend. What do you think of that?" (Keep in mind that the attitudes, discernment, pacing, and infatuation you display are teaching your children boundaries and how to respond in their own dating relationships.)

Engage in activities the kids enjoy, but don't make it one big sell job. Try to relax and let relationships develop on their own timing.

If the other person also has children, it might be wise to orchestrate early get-togethers with just one set of children. You might, for example, engage in an activity with your partner and their children one weekend and then have your partner join you and your kids the next. Navigating multiple new relationships can be overwhelming. Breaking the two families into parts can be helpful initially. Eventually, though, assuming your dating relationship continues to deepen, you'll want to get everyone together for shared activities.[1]

The Ex-Factor

Should you tell your children's other parent that you're dating, and if so, when? Good question. Before I address it, let me speak to the reaction some of you just had that sounded like, "It's none of my ex's business if I'm dating." Yes it is. Your relationship with another person has significance for the well-being of your children; therefore, your ex should care about the influence your dating partner will bring to the kids. (I'm sure you care who your ex dates.) No, it's not their decision who you date, but they do have an investment in your decisions.

The question of whether you tell your ex and how is a judgment call only you can make. The context of your co-parenting relationship and divorce will dictate whether this is a good idea or one that might cause excessive conflict. At some point, such as when you get married, they have to know. Whether you tell them early in the dating relationship or when it's serious is up to you. But keep this in mind: If you don't tell them, your kids might be forced to.

Talk with your kids about what they would say if the other parent asks if you are dating anyone. Some kids will feel fine answering—and they'll freely share how they feel about it. But for other kids, the question will make them uncomfortable. If it's extremely awkward or anxiety-producing for them to envision how they would handle the situation, empower them with this response: "I'm not the one to ask about that; I would prefer that you ask Mom/Dad directly." Essentially, the only way to help your children deal with the anxiety of this situation is to de-triangulate them. Not answering and inviting the other parent to speak to you directly takes your kids out of the middle.

The More You Push, the More Kids Push Back

Pushing children toward acceptance of your couple relationship, or expressing disappointment that they are not showing affection toward a dating partner or their children on your timetable, is likely to increase a child's resistance. Respect and relationship are earned, not demanded.

Expect Hot/Cold Reactions

Liking a parent's dating partner sometimes creates a loyalty problem for kids; they don't know how to embrace everyone and not hurt feelings (especially the other biological parent). Because they are caught in a loyalty conflict, children sometimes warm up nicely to a dating partner and then turn cold. Sometimes they vacillate. Don't panic or judge the children too harshly. Confusion comes with the territory. Relax and work with what they give you.

Hear Their Sadness

Biological parents in particular need to show that they are able to hear their children's sadness. Handle it with compassion, not self-pity or criticism. Doing so affirms that you can separate your desire for a partner from their desire for stability. If, on the other hand, you get defensive and hurt in response to their sadness, they may think they've lost you to your new love. Remember, sadness is rooted in fear.

THE BENEFITS OF FEAR

Well, there you have it: Two chapters on the sabotaging nature of fear. Pretty depressing, huh? What if I now told you that fear has benefits?

God uses the fearful places in life to grow us, to mature us. I'm not saying he creates the fear (although sometimes he might), but I am saying he uses the uncertain, anxious moments of life to teach us to trust him.

> ### Kids Talk
>
> "At first my thirteen-year-old was very territorial over me. It took a few months for him to get over it. I had to really reassure him nobody would ever take his place in my heart."—Jenny

"Consider it pure joy, my brothers and sisters, whenever you face trials of many kinds, because you know that the testing of your faith produces perseverance. Let perseverance finish its work so that you may be mature and complete, not lacking anything" (James 1:2–4). The half-brother of Jesus (were they a stepfamily?) wants us to know that trials and tough circumstances mature us. It's there, in the deep water, that God reminds us that we can rely on him. It's there, in darkness, that we realize how small we really are and how great is our need for his strength to press on. And it's there, in the not-knowing moments, that we develop perseverance, maturity, and greater trust.

Don't run from your fear, and try to encourage your children not to, either. Rather, find God in it.

Discussion Questions

1. React to this statement: Some children are excited for a parent to begin dating, others go into a jealous rage, but nearly all kids are concerned to some degree.

2. In children, each loss creates the fear of more loss, which in turn creates a sensitivity to anything that resembles loss, especially losses that involve parents and family members. Family attachments are highly prized by children under normal circumstances, but after loss, they are golden. When a parent dates, kids feel the shift in direction away from them and the family; this ignites their fear of more loss.

   - Make a list of the losses your children (or your dating partner's children) have experienced. Writing out this list, as opposed to just saying it, is important.

   - What fears have you already noticed in your children?

3. What did you learn from David and Donna's story?

4. What is the current speed and trajectory of your couple rocket headed toward Passion Planet? What is the speed and trajectory of the kids' rocket toward Maybe Moon? What is the difference between the two rockets?

5. Single parent: In what ways do you reassure your children of your continued presence, love, and commitment?

6. Describe any "What if?" conversations you may have had. If you haven't started these yet, what's the next step to begin doing so?

7. If we could ask your children how open you have been in the past to their fears (without defensiveness) and how helpful you are in labeling their emotions and coaching them through those emotions, what would they say?

8. Would your kids say that you've pushed an acceptance agenda ("I need you to like this person")?

9. Until you are serious, what is the advantage of spending special days and holidays *without* the dating partner?

10. Why is staying patient so important?

11. How would you know if your child needed you to postpone dating?

12. Review the Do's and Don'ts Guidelines starting on page 98. Which are pertinent to you?

Going Fishing

There's a rumor that there are more fish in the sea. If that's true, in order to catch one you'll have to go fishing. But how? What bait will you use? What type of fish are you looking for? In what part of the ocean will you let out your line? And once you hook one, how will you know if it's a good catch?

This next section will walk you through this labyrinth of dating decisions and help you make wise choices.

Chapter 6

Finding Love in All the Right Places . . . and in All the Right Ways

I was not married to a Christian my first time around. I learned that I needed a strong Christian man; I wouldn't date just anyone.

—Tammy, mom and stepmom

Since you could find a potential mate anywhere, this chapter is really more about *how* to look for someone worthy of marriage than *where*. That is the point, remember? Finding someone worthy of marriage—not just someone to have coffee with—is what you're after. Getting yourself ready is step one. Smart dating is step two.

ARTICULATE YOUR SILHOUETTE

When boy meets girl—and boy falls in love with girl—there is a lot of chemistry that is visible to any observer: extended smiles, gazing at each other, gestures that communicate an openness to each other, elation when you hear from them, random acts of kindness, and the like. But there is also a great deal of chemistry going on internally that no one can see. It centers in a tiny sector near the base of the brain called the ventral tegmental area. This area produces dopamine and sends it to many regions of the brain, especially the brain's reward system, which produces want, motivation, goal-oriented behavior, energy, and elation. "So, when you fall madly in love with someone, the brain is producing dopamine, a natural stimulant, to give you the focus, energy, elation, and motivation to win life's greatest prize—a mating partner."[1]

> **Best Practices Dating Tip**
>
> Be authentic right from the start even if it means revealing something unattractive about you. If you hide all your faults, you become fearful that you have to keep up the façade or lose their favor. Don't set yourself up to perpetually lie.

But here's the downside. This cocktail of biochemistry and highly motivated behavior is also clouding your judgment about the viability of your selection. Love is blind, remember? That's why you need a standard to measure this person by—a silhouette of substance to temper your dopamine-addicted high from your latest love interest. You need something to help you get below the surface of biochemistry and the many ways people make themselves look good. Plus, when someone measures up, you'll have confidence that the person you are dating is worth at least a temporary investment—and perhaps an eternal investment—of your life and the lives of the children.

By using the word *silhouette*, you might assume I mean the physical outline or bodily shape of the kind of person you are looking for. I do not. You can't judge a book by its cover, nor determine love based on physical accoutrements. (I've got bad news: All of life is a downward slide away from physical beauty—get used to it!) I'm suggesting you articulate a silhouette of someone's spirit, character, and inner beauty. That won't slide toward ugliness— ever! More important, successfully making a stepfamily a family requires emotional maturity, a strong sense of personal worth (in

Jesus Christ), and a spirit of humility to face all that can't be controlled (e.g., ex-spouses, a child who refuses to bond, etc.).

Let me be candid: The blended family is no place for emotionally weak, wimpy, or needy adults. As a single parent, if you date someone who is self-absorbed or has a strong need to be the emotional center of the home, you and your kids may be in for trouble. If you're single without children and you date a single parent who is emotionally fragile or paralyzed as a parent by guilt, you'll likely live a family nightmare. Date someone who is rigid and stubborn and you'll find yourself lonelier while married than you ever were while single. Find someone who is strong in character and emotionally stable.

> "I am looking for someone who puts God first in their life and prays with the children. He should be a good family man, an involved parent, a good provider, a good communicator, someone who puts others first, and has a good moral track record."—Kerry

His/Her Silhouette

If I may, allow me to suggest some personal character qualities that you should include in your silhouette. I'll let you decide whether it's important that they enjoy sushi.

Submissive to God. A person of faith is not the same as someone who attends church. Just because you're in a garage doesn't make you a car. Look for a follower of Christ, not just a fan of Christ who joins the masses of spectator Christians who gather every week to cheer on their pastor. But how will you know the difference, you ask? Look at their fruit. If they are a follower, it will show up in how they spend their money, the people they hang out with, the values they hold dear in their home, and the boundaries they set for their children. It is very easy to witness the overflow of submission in someone's heart—you just have to look past the outward façades most of us display in public and look at their real life. It will be a testimony either for submissiveness or selfishness. It's a very important distinction.

Humble. In every season of life, humility is the posture that acknowledges our dependence upon God and opens us to the sanctifying work of the Holy Spirit. From the moment we declare the lordship of Jesus till he comes again and "every knee shall bow," it is what prepares us to be transformed. Humility primes the canvas of the heart to receive the Holy Spirit's paint so we can more profoundly reflect the image of Christ. You may not marry a perfect person, but if you find a humble person, they will become increasingly perfect throughout their lifetime—and it will be a joy, not a burden, to walk beside them as they do.

So how can you recognize humility? While dating, most people are vigilant to put their best foot forward in order to impress the other person. But a humble person won't shy away from admitting their faults, even before they've won your heart. They are able to laugh at themselves (not take themselves too seriously), openly discuss their temptations and failings, and regularly call on the grace of God to redeem them from themselves. They don't need to appear attractive just to win your approval, because a humble person has their identity firmly planted in their relationship with God. Because they have God-esteem, they can be authentic with you. This is a supreme quality for marriage and family relationships. Pursue it in yourself and seek out a partner who is rich in it.

Sexually Controlled. This is a great litmus test of someone's submission to God. God made us sexual beings and purposed sex in marriage, in part, as a celebration and seal of the covenant between husband and wife. Every couple faces sexual temptation during courtship; dating someone who is tempted sexually doesn't tell you anything about the person. But someone who actively

> ### Kid Reactions
>
> "They didn't like the idea of my dating and getting to know people. They wanted me to find one man and exclusively date him. We've had lots of discussions about finding the right fit, what a godly man looks like, and who is worthy of dating. My son very much accepts my boyfriend. My daughter has the 'he's not my dad' attitude."

guards their heart from pre-covenant sexual behavior is revealing their submissiveness to God, their desire for a healthy relationship, and their respect for you. A person, on the other hand, who constantly pursues and pressures their partner sexually is showing that they don't possess much spiritual maturity. Pressuring behavior is a litmus test of character. Listen to what it is telling you about the person. (I'll talk more about managing sexual temptation later.)

A Spiritual Personal Trainer. Personal trainers are people who push us to get physically fit. They cheer us on our way to health. The silhouette of the person you are looking for includes someone who challenges your walk with the Lord. If they are chasing after God, just hanging out with them will inspire you to do the same.

In addition, personal trainers challenge us to put off unhealthy habits and put on better ones. Listen to the apostle Paul, personal trainer extraordinaire, laying out a healthy plan for living. Isn't this a good list of what to look for in a dating partner?

Put to death, therefore, whatever belongs to your earthly nature: sexual immorality, impurity, lust, evil desires and greed, which is idolatry. Because of these, the wrath of God is coming. You used to walk in these ways, in the life you once lived. But now you must also rid yourselves of all such things as these: anger, rage, malice, slander, and filthy language from your lips. Do not lie to each other, since you have taken off your old self with its practices and have put on the new self, which is being renewed in knowledge in the image of its Creator. . . .

Therefore, as God's chosen people, holy and dearly loved, clothe yourselves with compassion, kindness, humility, gentleness and patience. Bear with each other and forgive one another if any of you has a grievance against someone. Forgive as the Lord forgave you. And over all these virtues put on love, which binds them all together in perfect unity.

Colossians 3:5–10, 12–14

Measure the people you date by this standard and you'll be looking for the right kind of person.

Family Silhouette

Your silhouette needs to be twofold. Not only should it describe qualities you are looking for in a person, but also the qualities you hope to create as a family. This will have implications for both the couple relationship and the family relationships. Most single parents have a silhouette for the person but neglect the family silhouette. I'm encouraging you to have one for both—and falling short in either should be a deal breaker.

Parenting Considerations. Far too many single parents fall in love and marry a person who is good marriage material but not good stepparent material. What stuns me as a therapist is how many biological parents have admitted to me behind closed doors that they knew their boy/girlfriend was not good parent material *before* they married but ignored their own intuition because they didn't want to live alone, were hungry for sex, or needed another income to provide for their kids. Really? Please don't sacrifice your kids on the altar of your anxiety or lust. And do not think you can marry a bad parent and turn them into a good one.

While dating, examine their potential role as a stepparent by learning about their parenting ideals and how they were parented (which is the parenting style most of us default to, or do just the opposite of). As you get more serious about your relationship, bring them into your parenting situations and watch how they process it and what they think should happen. You are looking for harmony between your basic approach to parenting and theirs. No two adults parent exactly the same, and yes, both of you will change and grow together as parents should you marry, but it is unwise to date someone with a vastly different parenting style from yours. Merging polar opposite styles is extremely difficult.

Can you know if someone will be a good stepparent? There are no guarantees. Again, time is your friend. Watch, for example, how your kids and they bond over time. Is your dating partner increasingly invested in your kids and getting to know them? Do they enjoy your kids or are they just an inconvenience to your couple time? Do they offer their humble input into parenting—even if it means pointing out a weakness in you—because they are striving to see the child grow in "wisdom and stature, and in favor with God and man" (Luke 2:52)? These are the qualities of a person willing to take on the tasks of stepparenting.

> Meaghan tried to communicate her nonnegotiables and expectations to her boyfriend, but every time she asked a "What if?" question regarding the children, he shut her down and said, "Let's not talk about the 'What ifs' until they become a reality." Less than a year into the marriage, the couple was in crisis and had filed for divorce. Don't ignore the "What if?" conversations.

If you are dating a parent, take note of their parenting as well as their children's behavior and attitudes. I've often said that an oppositional child is a yellow caution light (sometimes a red stoplight) to dating the parent. I'm not blaming the parent for everything the child does, but it is an indicator that you should pay attention to. If nothing else, know that merging your life and kids with a conflictual or chaotic family situation over which you will have very little influence or control will bring anger and stress to your family life.

In addition, our daily lifestyle and how we go about living together under the same roof are primarily determined by parenting expectations. If your children are expected to clean up after themselves and contribute to household chores, but your dating partner's kids don't feel comfortable at home unless there are piles of clothes on the floor, you should take note of it. Don't minimize this dynamic. I know clothes on the floor are not a big deal, but multiply this dynamic by a hundred similar scenarios, and it will be—fast! Your kids will scream "not fair" and the stepkids will holler "foul" and you and your new spouse will find yourselves defending your kids and your preferences, only to end up on opposites sides of the issue—and your marriage. You have to consider the entire package when dating, not just the couple dynamic.

In my experience, people without children who are dating single parents are tempted to repeatedly minimize the parenting deficits of their dating partner. It's just too easy to think it's not significant. Please don't fall into this trap. Once married, you're going to be powerless to change what the kids' parent is unwilling to change, and you'll get tired of having to accommodate their irresponsibility really fast. I'll talk more about this caution light in chapter 7, but for now, make sure your silhouette includes dating a competent, healthy parent.

Best Practices Dating Tip

If the parenting of the other person is poor, don't think that you can fix their kids after marriage. It's very unlikely. Plus, if the person isn't motivated to be a better parent while single, they probably won't be after marriage, either. Attend parenting classes together, read books, and discuss better parenting, but if they don't improve, don't move toward marriage.

The Family Package. In addition to parenting matters, the blended family package includes—just to name a few— ex-spouses, the family loss story, financial stress and changes, former in-laws/grandparents, the parenting of the parent and stepparent in the children's other home, and the spiritual influences of former and current church leaders. You must carefully look into all of this, which will take time, but remember, time is your friend. If you can't marry the package—the *entire* package—then don't marry the person.

Family History and Patterns. As you grow increasingly serious about someone, be sure to visit their family of origin and learn about their family history. Who someone is becoming is often tied to who they came from. Do they have a history of close family connections, or are they disengaged and angry? Is there a generational pattern of chemical abuse or other addictions? That doesn't mean the person you are dating will be an addict (thank

God his grace redeems us from such things), but it may mean strained family relationships and irresponsible extended family members who will complicate your life. What is the story of faith in their extended family, and is it celebrated as the compass for life? How do men and women treat one another in their family, husbands and wives, parents and children? Bottom line: If you don't like their family, think seriously about not marrying into it.

Melissa has given a lot of thought to her silhouette:

I'm looking for someone who, initially, can respect my decision not to introduce my children to them for quite a while. I want someone whose parenting style (or their views on parenting if they don't already have children) closely resembles mine so that we are more likely to be able to present a united front in parenting. The person needs to be able to recognize their own flaws and be willing to address them as well as lovingly point out mine and help me address mine. The person should be patient and kind and willing (as things get serious) to be a supportive role model for my children, but not attempt to take the place of their father. He should speak well of me and not allow the kids to be disrespectful. By the same token, he should be respectful of their father's position and not speak ill of him. I've looked online, in church, at social events, and through friends to find someone like this. They are few and far between, but I believe they do exist.

Okay, Melissa, if they do exist, where are they? How does one find them?

ON MEETING SOMEONE

I'm less concerned about where you meet someone than how you manage your dating experience and expectations once you do. It seems to me that you never know when or where you'll meet someone of interest to you. A friend may introduce you to someone; you may bump into someone at church; or a chance meeting may change your life forever. It happens. Having said that, I do think there are wise ways and places to look for dates.

How to Look

Every year businesses spend millions trying to create places for singles to meet and fall in love. If I knew the secret to finding someone, I'd be rich. I don't and I'm not. But I can suggest that looking begins with perspective about the eternal purpose of finding a mate, then letting that perspective dictate where you look. Suppose, for example, you prayed the Dater's Prayer in faith each day:

Lord, work out your kingdom agenda in me. I am yours. If you bring someone into my life who submits to your will and will help me to love you more, then let that person be evident to me; let me not miss your provision. And if not, let me be content with your provision and at ease in my singleness.

Praying that prayer each day would help to relax your heart about finding a mate. You wouldn't over-desire finding someone and you wouldn't under-desire it. You would walk by faith with a sense of calm about your life.

Desperate singles look for love in the same places as content singles, but they ignore warning signs and make it their agenda to find "the one." Instead, make it God's agenda and then relax. You can still implement the below strategies, but you won't be desperate when doing so. Discernment will still have voice.

Where to Look

The Dater's Prayer positions your heart to be open to the people God brings to you. I've talked with many singles whose external, physical silhouette is so GQ-ish or Victoria's Secret-ish that they quickly discount the normal people in their lives. Are your standards so high that you look past people of high character but average beauty? Don't be quick to dismiss someone. Get to know the person on the inside first.

Look for dates in gatherings of people you generally know something about and that reflect your core values. Meeting someone during a service project or recreational activity or at church are good examples. Meeting someone at the national swingers convention is not (remind me sometime to tell you about the weekend when a church I was speaking at put me and my then ten-year-old son, Connor, up in a hotel that was hosting just such a gathering!). Let the venue do some of the filtering for you, but keep in mind that everyone can present themselves as something they're not—even (or should I say, especially) in church!

Also, I know it sounds old-fashioned, but ask your family, friends, or community of faith to suggest people they think would be a good fit for you. After all, they know you well and often have a decent perspective about who might fit your personality and interests. Perhaps this will give you a running start on finding someone.

Finally, don't try to suggest to someone that God told you they are your soul mate. As one man told the woman who said that to him, "Well, I'm pretty sure God's not going to leave me in the dark. If he told you that, he should be telling me—and I'm not hearing that from him." I call this using the Holy Spirit hammer; hit someone over the head with it and they're sure to fall in love with you . . . or not. Honestly, it just makes you look desperate and manipulative. That's not what they call *attractive*.

Online Dating: What Match.com and eHarmony Likely Won't Tell You

I must share some apprehensions with you about online dating. I realize that millions of people use online dating sites to help them meet someone. I do think that some sites, especially those that use proven psychological assessments, do give you a running start toward connecting with someone. That I find valuable for you. But I must point out a number of cautions for single parents that aren't necessarily true for those without kids, considerations that the online matchmakers will not share with you.

Couple vs. Family Satisfaction. Online dating sites are about helping you find a compatible person to date. The major premise of this book is that coupleness is one thing but familyness is another; online dating may give you a leg up on the former, but it doesn't speak to the latter.

In our book *The Remarriage Checkup*, Dr. Olson and I report that our research confirmed what family therapists have speculated for years: Before marriage, couple satisfaction is mainly tied to couple relationship factors, but after the wedding, couple satisfaction is increasingly tied to factors related to blended family harmony or the lack thereof. In other words, when it comes to blended family marriages, what happens between you is what makes you fall in love with someone, but what happens around you (e.g., stepparent-stepchild issues, ex-spouse pressures, step-family disharmony, etc.) is increasingly responsible for what creates couple distress and divorce.

Don't let an online dating service lull you into thinking that the person who is right for you is right for your kids and family.

Long-distance Romance. Dating online increases the likelihood that the person you meet lives elsewhere. I have coached many dating couples who live across the country from each other, even one couple that lived on opposite sides of the planet. Here's the problem: Long-distance romances mature into logistical nightmares for parents and children.

Jeremy wrote me, "We are looking for resources to try and decide whether to move my fiancée eight hundred miles from Kansas with her resistant soon-to-be high school daughter to be closer to me in Pennsylvania. Her daughter has few school friends. We are struggling as to what would be best for all involved and want to be a successful stepfamily in the future!" Well, Jeremy, finding what's "best for all" assumes that what's best for you as a couple will also be best for a resistant teenager. That's a big assumption—and a big risk.

I even had one couple email me saying they had married but thought they could continue a long-distance marriage. It wasn't working out so they wanted me to fix in a day what they hadn't been able to resolve. "I was wondering if you have an opening this coming Saturday. My husband lives in Michigan and I live in Houston. We have been married for one year (a second marriage for both of us), and we have been arguing about who needs to relocate. I am at the point of giving up on this marriage, but I want to try a counseling session first instead of having our usual never-ending discussion about this."

> **Best Practices Dating Tip**
>
> Don't be afraid to ask the tough questions. And what are they? Whatever you find yourself avoiding in order not to rock the boat.

Let me be frank. Falling in love with someone long-distance is very complicated and in most cases downright lousy for kids (unless they are very young). First of all, it makes getting to know each other very difficult and doesn't help you to assess the fit of your dating partner and kids. Second, know that moving kids to a new town while launching a new family at the same time is double trouble. They have a new family, new school, lost friends, lost community connections, lost church, etc. It requires a tremendous amount from the kids, so unless they absolutely love the notion, it's a bad idea for everyone involved.

Should logistics temper your decision to date someone long-distance? Yes. Does it ever work out well? I've only known of a few, and most of them were when a person without children moved to where the children lived. If you insist on dating someone long-distance, think ahead and moderate your investment in them with awareness of what it will likely cost your children later on if the relationship continues.

Hiding Your True Self. Online it's very easy to appear to be someone you're not. This is true for a number of reasons. First, everyone puts their best foot forward when dating in person; even more so, the format of online chat, website postings, replying to emails and texts, etc., allows you and your dating interest to carefully and methodically choose your responses. Emotion is suppressed and rational, well-thought-out replies are crafted. It's not that people are lying, they're just choosing carefully how you will view them. But then again, sometimes people do lie.

USA Today reported on a poll asking, "How honest are you on your social networking sites?" Almost one-third said they were totally honest, 26 percent fibbed a little, 21 percent said what they posted about themselves was a total fabrication, and 22 percent admitted to flat-out lying.[2] Adding it up, 69 percent said they were untruthful. Yikes.

Online dating can be a helpful jump start to a relationship, but be sure you verify in person everything you come to believe about someone through online interaction. (See Appendix 1 for tips on safe social networking.)

DATING BEST PRACTICES . . . AND ATTITUDES

I've gathered more collective wisdom from my dating single parent focus group and summarized some of their best practices for you here.

Define the Relationship

Steve shared, "On our first date, the woman who would become my wife asked me, 'So, what do you want from this relationship?' Being the self-centered, nervous, just-trying-not-to-look-stupid-on-the-first-date guy that I was, I had no idea how to answer her. I hadn't thought past the next five minutes, let alone the future of our relationship. Awkward! But in hindsight, what I then thought was a silly question turned out to be a really good one."

Defining the relationship (or DTR) means that you and the person you are dating express your intentions to each other, and you do so each time the relationship moves to a new level. You don't have to pop the "What are you looking for?" question on the first date, but fairly soon it is helpful to make this overt with each other. Couples often assume they know what the other person's intentions are and then are surprised when they realize they were wrong.

In the beginning you want to know: Do you only date people who are marriageable, or will you keep dating someone that you'd never consider for marriage? Are you just trying to get out of the house, or are you actively looking for a mate? Questions like these define the nature and intent of your relationship and give both parties the information they need to determine if they want to keep seeing the other.

Kid Reactions

"Mason is happy to have Keith in our lives and looks forward to us getting married. He is encouraging us to get engaged."

After a few initial dates, DTR again. "I've really enjoyed getting to know you and I'd like us to become more intentional about learning about each other. Do you agree? Do you think we're ready to, for example, learn more about each other's values and life goals? I'm thinking we need to start spending more time with each other's kids, too. What do you think?"

Another DTR dialogue is one that sounds like this: "I am interested in us enough to make this an exclusive dating relationship. How do you feel about that?" You can then discuss the boundaries around your relationship and expectations for each other. These then form the guidelines for the next season of your dating. Eventually you may find it's time for this DTR discussion: "I am beginning to see us getting married. I'm wondering if you are entertaining that idea, as well." Notice, this is not "Do you want to get engaged?" This is "Are you open to considering engagement?"

This kind of intentional dialogue helps both people track the status of their relationship and adds security when the relationship is defined—even when the two people are at different places. For example, should one partner be ready for engagement and the other not, the "ready" partner will be disappointed, but at least both people know where they stand.

By the way, if both people agree that they are ready to consider engagement, the next topics of conversation should be, "Are the kids ready for us to do that?" and "What steps do we need to take to aid the trajectory of that rocket?"

Engagement and marriage are the ultimate DTR moments. They confirm to the couple that they intend to marry and announce to the world that a new family is beginning. These signposts are easily identified in our culture. But the DTR principle is just as important at the beginning and middle stages of dating. Don't be afraid of bringing it up.

Slow Down

Falling in love creates an anesthetic that numbs your common sense. Be aware of this enough to slow down your dating and spend at least a year of face-to-face time with someone. This allows the anesthetic to wear off so your discernment can be clear.

Maintain Sexual Purity

Before marriage, love is blind and sex is a blindfold. Charles and Diana (not their real names, but it does make the story more interesting) scheduled a consult with their counselor to discuss their dating relationship. Diana had two children from a previous marriage and Charles had never been married before. They had been dating for seven years, and their therapist soon found out why they hadn't pulled the trigger on marriage.

Charles and Diana had been raised in two totally different parenting systems. Charles was raised in a strict, conservative home. Diana grew up in a chaotic family where you never knew what was going to happen next. There were few boundaries, little discipline, and a lot of freedom (which Diana was more than happy to take advantage of during her teen years). Now a parent herself, Diana was parenting her children, ages eighteen and nine, the same way she had been parented.

> **Best Practices Dating Tip**
>
> Talk to others who know the person. Get objective feedback from their friends and family members.

Charles and Diana had constant conflict over her parenting and her children's behavior. Charles protested that they got away with murder and suggested Diana step up her expectations or they would waste their lives away in irresponsibility. Diana disagreed. To her, keeping the children happy and at peace with her was more important than drawing tough lines in the sand.

Given this stalemate, you might be wondering why in the world this couple was still together. Their counselor was, too. When all these differences were laid out before the couple and they were asked why they thought they hadn't broken up, an honest answer came forth: sex. They were sexually active on a regular basis, and no matter what they fought about, sex brought them back together. In other words, if it wasn't for sex, they wouldn't have anything. Sex was their blindfold.

Both Charles and Diana believed that ideally sex should be reserved for marriage. When asked why she would continue to intertwine her life with a man who could be so black-and-white judgmental about her parenting but gray when it came to denying himself sex with her, Diana just shrugged her shoulders. And when asked why he continued to date Diana even though time had proven to him that she was not interested in changing her parenting (only he was motivated to change her parenting), Charles couldn't come up with an answer. Both Charles and Diana had attached themselves to a fantasy image of one another; sex and emotional immaturity had blinded them to this truth.

Keeping in mind that this couple was dating and arguing over the same issue for seven years when they came for their consultation, if you were their counselor, what would you have said to them when asked, "Should we stay together?"

Managing Sexual Temptation. God knows what a powerful force sexuality is in our lives. After all, he designed it. God is very much invested in your sexual fulfillment. That's why he placed boundaries around sex; he knows in a marital context how beneficial sex can be, and he knows how problematic it can be in a dating relationship. Charles and Diana, for example, had very little foundation to their relationship, and yet sex fooled them into thinking they had more in the bank than they really did. Physiologically we can explain it this way: The hormone oxytocin, sometimes called the "cuddle hormone," facilitates bonding in mammals (e.g., between a mother and her newborn child). It is also released when couples are affectionate and escalates dramatically after orgasm, especially in men. In short, it makes you feel connected even when there is no substance to a relationship. Charles and Diana were writing checks with their lives based on a bankrupt account. In the end, they got hurt and wasted a lot of time on a quick but shallow high.

Maintaining a desire for the best in your life—and in your future marriage—starts by trusting that God has your best interest in mind. By declaring sexuality before marriage a sin, he is not being a simpleton or killjoy; he is trying to protect you from a shallow relationship and personal pain. The only question is, do you trust his motives and his insight? Before marriage, sex tends to be about what we can get from the other person. Sex that is saved until after marriage has time to mature into a physical and soul expression of the deep foundation of the relationship that has already been established and the life-long commitment expressed to each other during the wedding. Saving sex till after marriage protects the objectivity of your dating, ripens your commitment to each other, and then as a symbol of marital oneness blossoms in a pleasurable celebration of love. That's worth waiting for.

> Karen's son was nearing his wedding day when he told his mother, "If you and Bill had slept together before marriage, Calli and I probably would have, too. But you didn't—so we didn't, either."

Practical Strategies for Managing Sexual Temptation. One day this phone message appeared on my desk: "Ron, please call L. S. He and his fiancée—they have only known each other two months—have been reading *The Smart Stepfamily* and are stumped by the suggestion of waiting two years to marry. It seems unreasonable to them that a passionate couple could wait two years before having sex. It's important to both him and his fiancée to manage their relationship with purity. BTW, they have nine children in all."

All couples are sexually tempted. Here are some practical tips for managing your temptations.

1. Get accountable. You must invite others to help you stay accountable to your goal of sexual purity. Giving a friend, pastor, family member—even your teenage or adult children—permission to randomly ask both of you about your behavior raises the bar and helps you to think of how your actions will be viewed by others.

2. Let God define sex. When someone says "Did you have sex?" what we usually hear is "Did you have *intercourse*?" That's unfortunate for many reasons. First, it implies that we can engage in all other forms of sexual touch (including oral sex and mutual manual stimulation to orgasm) and think we haven't "had sex." Second, it lulls us to sleep about how far we can go and still be safe (see item 4 below). And third, it turns sexuality into a legalistic game of avoiding sin rather than a spiritual matter of trust and discipleship.

Ephesians 5:3 says, "There must not be even a hint of sexual immorality, or of any kind of impurity, or of greed, because these are improper for God's holy people." Sexual immorality there is defined specifically as fornication or intercourse. But Ephesians 4:19 broadens the definition of sex to include sensual behavior (e.g., loose conduct, unchaste behavior, lust) that starts long before intercourse. "Having lost all sensitivity, they have given themselves over to sensuality so as to indulge in every kind of impurity."

The issue here is not "Can we touch here or there?" The issue is bringing our sexual passions under the lordship of Christ. It's not, "How close to the edge can we stand?" but "How can we honor Christ with our behavior?" That is a far greater challenge, but one worth every effort.

3. View how you and your dating partner manage sexuality as a spiritual precedent for your marriage. Erin and Josh committed themselves to purity. But Erin's continual efforts to introduce sex to their relationship educated Josh on her spiritual maturity. He listened to what her lack of discipline was telling him about her, and it helped him to look past her outward appearance. Plus, he knew that if he couldn't provide spiritual leadership now, he would struggle to do so in their marriage. In the end, because Erin and Josh couldn't unite over this matter, Josh broke off the relationship.

4. Agree to a Purity Covenant. Couples who can't talk about their sexual temptations are destined to fall prey to them. But don't just acknowledge them, discuss the values behind purity and agree to a plan. Consider drafting a written purity covenant (a sample is available in Appendix 2) that details your values and plan. This is an excellent teaching and modeling tool for your children, too. When the time is appropriate, show them this document and say, "This is what we did and this is what we would encourage you to do, as well."

5. Understand that there's no reverse in sex. Have you noticed that sex only has a forward gear? Once you break a certain touch barrier, you'll quickly return to it and will never be satisfied backing up. In other words, take very seriously any forward movement. Even benign affectionate touch that is meant to communicate connection and love moves us further toward sexual touch that is arousing. Be careful not to awaken love before its time (Song of Solomon 2:7). Embrace God's definition of sex and then ask yourself where you need to stop in order not to cross into sensuality. You might also think of it this way. Picture your dating partner having a Hula-Hoop around them. Every time you enter the hoop, you make physical touch the focus of interaction and you lose objectivity in the relationship. Stay outside the hoop as much as you can.

6. Date in public. Being in a private place (e.g., home, hotel, or car) explodes sexual temptation because no one is watching. On the other hand, I've never seen a couple having sex on a table in McDonald's.

> **Best Practices Dating Tip**
>
> Don't ignore the flashing yellow caution lights, and don't run red lights! (See chapter 7.)

7. Date in a group. Being with other couples adds accountability, but it also offers objectivity. Again, when you enter each other's Hula-Hoop, you stop assessing the person, their values, and your fit together as a couple and start focusing on physical and sexual touch. Being in a group helps you stay outside the hoop and also brings perspective as you consider this person through the eyes of others you trust.

8. Don't live together. In the next chapter I'll share in detail why doing so breeds insecurity in a relationship, but for now recognize that cohabitation will most certainly sexualize your relationship.

Discussion Questions

1. Write down the silhouette of the person you are looking for.

2. If you are currently dating, review my recommended silhouette qualities in light of the person you are dating (rate them from 1 to 10). If not currently dating, consider previous partners and how well these qualities describe them.

   - Submissive to God

   - Humble

   - Sexually controlled

   - A spiritual personal trainer

3. Now consider the family silhouette you desire and the qualities discussed on pages 122–125.

   - Parenting

   - The family package

   - Family history and patterns

4. How would praying the Dater's Prayer every day change how you date?

Lord, work out your kingdom agenda in me. I am yours. If you bring someone into my life who submits to your will and will help me to love you more, then let that person be evident to me; let me not miss your provision. And if not, let me be content with your provision and at ease in my singleness.

5. Where have you been looking for dates? What will you do differently after reading this chapter?

6. Articulate the limitations of online dating. (This doesn't mean you shouldn't try it, just be aware of the unique weaknesses for single parents.)

7. What challenges does long-distance dating present?

8. In the past, how proactive have you been in defining the relationship (DTR)? What challenges or fears does DTR bring to you?

9. Discuss the matter of sexual purity. What do you believe is God's desire for your relationship?

10. If dating, outline and discuss together how you intend to maintain purity. If not dating, discuss which suggestions in this chapter would be helpful to you in the future.

Chapter 7

Yellow Light. Red Light. Green Light.

My ex-boyfriend used to talk about what he liked about his ex-girlfriend's body. That would be why he's my ex-boyfriend.

Gail

Choose your rut carefully. You'll be in it for the next 200 miles.

Road sign in Alaska

Troy and Meredith had been dating off and on for six years. They had lived together for a time, but were separated when they came to their first session. Both had been married before, but only Meredith had children. "We're trying to figure out if we have anything to salvage," they shared. "We love each other but just don't seem to like each other very much." I immediately thought of the research I shared in chapter 1 about couples who date longer than five years having more relationship issues than other couples. I thought, *It's likely both for some reason are afraid of being hurt.* Sure enough, I was right. Troy and Meredith had some core trust issues that resulted in a merry-go-round, on-and-off relationship with neither feeling confident about the future.

Troy had lead Meredith to the Lord early in their relationship, and while he saw many changes in her behavior, he couldn't help but fear her chaotic childhood and how it had turned her to drugs at one point in her life. Even though she had been clean for four years, he told me she still had an addictive personality and he just couldn't trust her.

Still trying to manage her addiction temptations, Meredith was afraid of herself, her history of poor choices, and Troy. "I am so grateful that he brought me to the Lord," she shared, "but he has slept with me ever since. How can I respect him on Sunday when he presses me for sex on Saturday?"

Both Troy and Meredith were seeing some yellow caution lights. Now what do they do?

TRAFFIC LIGHTS

Traffic lights are meant for our safety. Flashing yellow lights alert us to take caution in moving forward. They demand that we slow down and take a careful look before proceeding. Once our hesitations are satisfied, we can move forward with greater confidence. Red lights, however, demand that we stop. And there's always good reason to stop at a red light, even if we can't immediately see it. Running it will likely result in being broadsided.

In dating there are two kinds of yellow and red lights: general and specific. General ones are usually true for all couples and tend to have more to do with circumstances or dynamics beyond your control. The openness of children to a future stepparent or how quickly someone begins dating after a breakup is a good example. Specific lights have to do with, for example, opposing personality characteristics in you and the person you are dating or contrasting values.

Troy and Meredith were experiencing specific flashing yellow lights and thankfully were not ignoring them. Despite how intertwined their lives had become over the past six years (which diminishes objectivity and makes us nearsighted), they were heeding the yellow lights and slowing down to ask the hard questions.

You should do the same.

This chapter does not present an exhaustive list of yellow and red lights. Some have already been presented. For example, dating someone who is not a Christ-follower is a red light; so is dating someone who is addicted to drugs or alcohol. Likewise, a yellow light flashes when you realize the other person is a poor parent (chapter 6), and a red one lights up if your, your children's, or your dating partner's fears are making trust impossible (chapters 4 and 5). We've already started the list; add these to it.

FLASHING YELLOW LIGHTS

Here are some common flashing yellow lights that should be heeded. After slowing down to take a good look around, check your level of confidence in the situation to see if the yellow light has turned green or red.

General Caution: Dating Is Inconsistent With Actual Blended Family Living[1]

This flashing yellow light essentially translates again into the "slow down" message. A lot of couple harmony during dating makes the road ahead appear clear and safe, but once you top the hill of marriage, you'll likely find some road hazards on the other side. Nearly everyone does.

Paul and Brenda know exactly what I'm talking about. Paul is senior pastor of a large metropolitan church in the Midwest. He had a wonderful twenty-seven-year marriage to his first wife, Karen, who tragically died of cancer. About a year before Karen passed away, one of Paul's best friends, Terry, died of cancer, as well. Terry's wife of twenty-five years, Brenda, had graciously cared for him throughout his battle with cancer. Six months after Karen's death and eighteen months after Terry's death, Paul and Brenda began dating. Paul had four children ranging from their early teens to mid-twenties, and Brenda had three children in the late teens and mid-twenties. After dating for less than a year, Paul and Brenda made plans to marry.

Five years into their remarriage, Paul asked me to come and speak to his congregation. A weekend stepfamily conference gave me the opportunity to hear more of their story and meet their friends Pamela and Allen, who were dating (both with children from previous marriages).

What fascinated me was the behind-the-scenes advice and coaching Paul and Brenda had given their friends Pamela and Allen. Before I share their advice, please understand that both Paul and Brenda are very high-functioning people and parents. They both had very good first marriages, both are educated professionals, and both had had success and joy in raising their children before their spouses passed away. In addition, since becoming widowed, they were quite intentional in grieving well and helping their children move through the loss of their parent. And since marrying and becoming a blended family, Paul and Brenda had led a stepfamily enrichment group at their church for a few years.

Despite all that, five years into their marriage, their blended family experience continued to be stressful and difficult. Their advice to their friends: Proceed with caution. One night over dinner I was honored to listen in as Paul and Brenda candidly shared with Pamela and Allen their newfound perspective about dating and becoming a blended family. "We love each other dearly, but if we had it to do all over again, we might not have gotten married at all." Paul and Brenda had by experience come face-to-face with the truth that coupleness does not equal familyness, and their 20/20 hindsight advice to their friends was direct and straightforward: *Don't rush into marriage. Make sure you are ready to marry the entire package that comes along with the person you have fallen in love with, or don't marry—and even if you are ready, keep in mind that there's no guarantee that doing so is best, convenient, or a blessing for your kids.* In other words, their advice was to step very carefully into a stepfamily because the love felt between the couple before the wedding does not predict family harmony after the wedding.

Sounds negative and discouraging, huh? Well, that depends on what you do with it. Pamela and Allen took their friends' advice to heart and delayed their wedding for well over a year so they could be more sensitive to the needs of their children and more adequately deepen their couple relationship before deciding for sure to marry. I caught up with Pamela sometime later and asked her to reflect on the advice they had received and their dating journey; here's what she shared:

> *Allen and I both affirm that waiting has enriched our relationship and allowed time for valuable relationship bridges to be built with our kids. This has also given our kids time to get used to the idea of our families eventually merging. Another hidden blessing of all this is that by the time we do marry, we will have a nearly empty nest (only one teenager left at home). Even so, I have concerns about what holidays will look like for our families.*
>
> *I must say, the waiting time has allowed us to move beyond the euphoric infatuation stage into the nitty-gritty hard places of loving each other. Facing those things before marriage is certainly healthier, enabling us to move forward without rose-colored glasses (to whatever degree that is possible). As I always tell my clients [Pamela is a licensed counselor herself], "Rose-colored glasses make red flags look pink!"*

Amen, sister. Amen.

General Caution: A Quick Turnaround

Do you remember in chapter 1 my discussion of the pit of pain and how it *pushes* us toward relationships, often without discernment? Dating someone who has recently gone through a painful experience but is now eager to be with you is dangerous. Their desperation and loneliness are flashing yellow lights. Perhaps they are still finalizing their divorce, just a few months past the death of a spouse, or recently broken up with a boyfriend or girlfriend and haven't let time be their healing friend. They are on the rebound and will likely bounce you into pain, too.

General Caution: Pressured to Marry and Willing to Accommodate

If you or the person you are dating is being pressured by friends and family members to marry, take a step back. Unfortunately, Christians can be the worst about this. Well-intentioned mothers, for example, who want their daughters to marry and have babies can push them to lower their standards and get hitched. Obviously, this adds undue pressure to the process of dating and sabotages discernment.

> ### Kids
>
> Because porn is so accessible, the average age that children are exposed to it is now eight. Be aware of how much access all the children have had.

Specific Caution: Pornography Use

The easy availability of pornography today means that dating parents should assume that anyone they date, male or female, has had some exposure to pornography. The question you should ask is not "Have you ever seen porn?" but "How much porn have you viewed?" I hate to say it, but if your dating partner claims they have never seen it, invite them to be more candid. "Honestly, I find that hard to believe. I want us to be able to share our temptations with each other, so I need you to be honest with me. If you'd like to revise your answer I'd appreciate it." The impact of porn can derail a marriage; you need to know what you're getting into. If they have ever habitually used pornography, this yellow light turns red.

Specific Caution: Character Issues

We all have failings and faults and dare I say character issues. Be sure to manage your own, and have both eyes open when it comes to seeing the other's. For example, some people are neat freaks who need their bed made, dishes put away, and toilet seats down before leaving the house. Others are obsessive compulsives who require that the floor be scrubbed with a mop each day, that Lysol be sprayed anytime someone sneezes, and can't walk out of a room—or let you walk out of the room—without checking twelve times that the light was turned off. Living with the first is one thing, the second something totally different.

Here are a few character matters not to ignore:

- a quick temper or intimidating, angry reactions
- a history of chemical abuse or physical violence[2]
- someone who can't say no to you (it sounds great on the surface but represents a fragile insecurity that will cause many problems later)
- someone who consistently blames others for their irresponsibility—an indication of pride or a fragile ego
- someone who won't honor or respect your boundaries. Forgetting is one thing (yellow light), but consistently pushing through without regard for your needs is a red light!
- someone who is Dr. Jekyll to you but Mr. Hyde to your kids (this is rated yellow only because it might be related to a kid's closed heart; if not, this turns red fast)
- someone who cannot calm themselves during conflict—a healthy partner manages their level of negative emotion so they can listen and respond, not overreact

- someone who has excessive debt from poor principled living or low self-control (income is not the issue here; poor self-control is, and it will play out in a million scenarios in a family)

- excessive enmeshment (blind closeness) or disengagement with their family of origin—typically this is an indication of strong control issues or negativity within the family. This can be culturally driven, as well; nevertheless, it's a compelling dynamic that should be embraced since you won't be able to change it (see the movie *My Big Fat Greek Wedding* for an example).

- someone who is deceptive or secretive about previous relationships—this includes someone who is always negative about a former spouse (to cast the other in a negative light is to attempt to make oneself always look good)

- a diagnosed personality disorder (e.g., bipolar, obsessive-compulsive, or borderline personality disorder)

The nature of falling in love is to minimize these matters. As time allows the anesthetic of romance to wear off, objectively ask yourself, since many of them probably won't change, whether you are willing to live with these or not.

Specific Caution: A Difficult or Unbelieving Ex-Spouse

We've already talked about the lack of wisdom of yoking oneself to an unbeliever, but why does it matter if their ex-spouse is an unbeliever? An unbelieving ex means your stepchildren will have many contrasting moral messages that will impact their behavior and attitudes. It may also be a sour and depressing dynamic for your spouse (who may feel frustrated in parenting their children and guilty about enjoying yours) and a constant "thorn in the flesh" to your family unit (e.g., if the children make decisions that bring about heartache). Plus it means your children may be exposed to many ungodly influences (a spiritual Trojan horse) that you cannot control. It is one thing to send our kids out into the world;

it's another to bring the world directly to them. It also means that prodigal living and parental heartbreak are more likely for all the children (which can be stressful on a marriage).

Brian and Linda didn't get any pre-stepfamily counseling because they thought they didn't have any issues with his children or their relationship. He had two girls ages nine and thirteen who loved getting to know Linda over their year-and-a-half dating period. "The girls made comments like, 'When are you two going to get married?'" she shared. It all seemed to be working out so well. But the moment they mentioned marriage, Brian's ex-wife went to work creating chaos. An angry alcoholic, she took the couple to court multiple times, costing them well over $50,000, every dime they had in savings. It was one nightmare after another.

This type of situation often makes us protest, "It's hard enough finding someone; it isn't fair that an ex should have that much impact on whether you date them or not!" or "But I'm not marrying them." You're right. But you are marrying the package, remember? Marriage to a divorced person means getting a mother-in-law, a father-in-law, and an ex-spouse-in-law. Therefore, you better weigh the consequences for you and your kids before doing so.

Specific Caution: Personality Differences

There's a maddening dynamic about the interplay of personalities. Before marriage, opposites attract, but after marriage opposites attack.

She was attracted to him because he was predictable and well-intentioned. A quiet, reserved man, he brought stability to her life. He loved that she knew how to have a good time. Well liked by many friends, she taught him how to laugh and be spontaneous. Now that they are married, many of their enduring disagreements center on these very issues. She accuses him of being boring, and he gets tired of her losing her car keys. She agrees to budget spending limits but then buys something on a whim; to keep them out of the poorhouse he feels like he has to parent her spending and she feels controlled by it.

The more your personality traits are similar, the easier it is to live with someone; the more different they are, the harder it is. As one insightful therapist noted, when you choose a partner, you are choosing a set of problems for life![3] (That reminds me of a sign seen beside an Alaskan highway that reads, "Choose your rut carefully. You'll be in it for the next 200 miles.") And since personality differences are the seed for many perpetual conflicts in marriage (69 percent of conflicts are about issues that will remain with the couple throughout their lives[4]), you better see clearly how the personality of the other intersects with yours. How can you do that?

Use the voucher code in the back of this book to take the Couple Checkup. The SCOPE section of the couple report will give you insight into your personalities and how they intersect. In addition, my book *The Remarriage Checkup*, coauthored with Dr. David Olson, discusses in depth how personalities harmonize or collide in marriage.

Personality differences are a double-edged sword. On one hand, they challenge us to grow as we realize our selfishness and how it impacts the other. On the other hand, extreme differences present repetitive occasions for conflict. Proceed with caution.

Specific Caution: Attempts to Meddle in the Other Person's Parent-Child Relationship

Sometimes future stepparents believe they can improve or modify the relationship between their dating partner and their child(ren). But beware: Nothing will sabotage a remarriage more quickly than one partner trying to rearrange the relationship of the other person and their child.[5] Meddling only results in polarization and conflict. This is the cardinal sin of blended families and will likely result in failure. Don't do it and don't attach yourself to someone who tries.

RED STOPLIGHTS

In case you've forgotten, a flashing yellow light means proceed with caution. A red light means *stop!*

"Let's Hurry and Get Married!"

I realize that "My life is complete now that I've met you. I can't live without you, let's get married . . . today!" makes for a great romance novel, but rarely does it make for a lifelong love. Don't be smitten by someone's strong desire to skip the process of dating (and, therefore, the process of discovering your fit, or lack thereof, as a couple and family). This usually indicates the person is desperate, insecure, and emotionally fragile—plus, it increases the chance that the children will feel thrown under the bus and resentful of the marriage.

Extreme Differences in Parenting

In the last chapter I noted that when adults have very different parenting styles, the marriage and family suffer (in particular when both adults bring children to the marriage). In my experience as a family therapist working with stepfamilies since 1993, I would say that this dynamic is the most common saboteur of blended marriages. Given that, it seems necessary to plainly repeat the caution here: Stop dating someone if you can't see eye to eye on parenting. I'll say more about this in chapter 8.

Someone Who Can't on Occasion Sit in the Backseat

Have you ever tried to have a friendship or relationship with someone who demanded to be the center of attention all the time? It's not much fun, huh? In a stepfamily, this same person will whine to no end.

I've often said that a blended family is no place for thin-skinned people. It's also not a place for adults who need to be at the center of the family (I like to call them "center babies"). Everyone in a stepfamily has to take the backseat every once in a while (especially stepparents); doing so helps bring grace to undefined relationships. It's pretty common for people to feel jealous and left out occasionally, but center babies won't put up with it and will attempt to control or manipulate the other relationships in the home to become the center of attention. If you find yourself dating this person, run for the hills.

Horrible Ex

If a difficult ex-spouse is a yellow light, a horrible ex is a red one. You have to decide which it is. Katy wrote to me saying, "My boyfriend has three boys ages eleven, nine, and four. Every time we make plans, their mom creates some sort of chaos and our plans have to change. I'm sure she does it on purpose." I'm sure you're right, Katy. And if you think it's bad now . . . wait till you get married.

Pseudo-Commitment: Settling for Cohabitation

Cohabitation has become so common it has changed the way people date. In many circles it is assumed that dating couples will eventually live together on their way to marriage. In fact, living together for many is considered another way to gauge the seriousness of the relationship; first you live together, then you get engaged. But is cohabitation healthy? No, it's not. Even dating someone who advocates for it is a red light. Let me make my case.

There is a great deal of research and debate today about the pros and cons of cohabiting. Of course, there is a spiritual side to this conversation related to sex outside of marriage, but since I've addressed that elsewhere (see chapter 6), I'd like to focus the conversation here on what social science has to say about cohabitation. Let's examine whether couple and family research lines up with God's wisdom for our lives. To start, let's think outside of the coupleness matters and consider the familyness issues. **Cohabitation is not good for kids.** For children, "the cohabiting stepfamily is the most dangerous family form in America today."[6] There are many reasons couples give for cohabiting: saving money, spending more time together, uncluttering their lives, and testing the relationship.[7] You'll notice that all of them are conveniences for the adults. But what isn't convenient is that children are put at risk when couples cohabit. Children face higher risks of abuse (physical, emotional, and sexual) and lower psychological well-being.[8] And they are exposed to numerous family transitions in and out of marriage and/or cohabitation, which in turn increase the likelihood of them having sex at an earlier age, having their first child out of wedlock, cohabiting before marriage, and having a lower confidence in the institution of marriage (which often translates into divorcing more quickly than previous generations).[9]

Perhaps most critically, I believe it dilutes the process of faith formation in children. When kids are exposed to multiple parental figures (for example, cohabiting stepparents) across both their homes, frequently they are presented with multiple religious worldviews.

A related negative outcome for single parents is that cohabitation deteriorates parental authority and makes their spiritual training weaker. Many adolescents have asked me essentially this question: "How can Mom tell me not to party when she moved us into his house before they were married?" Parents who want children who live by God's moral standards must themselves live by those same standards, no matter how impractical they may be. In short, cohabitation doesn't benefit your kids, especially not if you're trying to create a home of safety, integrity, and clear moral standards.

Cohabitation is not healthy for the couple relationship. Forty-six percent of young adults believe that "living together would improve their chances for a good marriage."[10] They are mistaken. I wish I could discuss this in more detail, but for the sake of space, let me sum up what the last decade of academic research has discovered about cohabiting couples (with some commentary). There is debate about whether cohabitation creates these effects or whether they arise out of characteristics of people who cohabit, but either way, the relationship suffers. Cohabiting couples:

- increase their risk of divorce by 50 percent (when ironically they are trying to protect themselves from hurt).
- value their independence rather than an interdependent relationship.[11] (You can't test a relationship by sitting on the side of the pool and dipping your toe in the shallow end—you have to jump into the deep end to know whether you can really swim.)
- are less sexually trustworthy.[12] (Marriage clearly removes other options.)
- have more negative attitudes about marriage[13] (which is one reason they avoid it).
- have lower religious commitment.[14] (Thirty percent of cohabiting people agree that doing so is against their own beliefs,[15] revealing the gap between their beliefs and actions.)
- sometimes exchange intentional dating for the pseudo-security of being together.[16] (They stop exploring their fit.)
- break up at a rate of 50 percent before marrying.[17] (Unfortunately, trial marriage often has a trial commitment.)
- have lower marital quality and commitment if they do marry (compared to couples who did not cohabit before marriage,[18] which makes them more vulnerable to pain).
- are tempted to "slide" into marriage ("We're living together and sharing a bus pass, why not get hitched?") instead of

making a conscious decision to throw their entire selves into marriage[19] (which firmly places both people in the deep end of the pool, swimming together).

Let me reiterate: All of the above are results from social science, but they clearly agree with God's boundaries around sexuality and what is best for us.

Someone who pushes for cohabitation is, I believe, telling you about their fear. Since they can't have a guarantee that marriage will last, they protect themselves with an arrangement that is marriage-like but without the legal bonds. They actually prefer the ambiguity of cohabitation ("we're together, sort-of") to the risk of rejection and a marriage gone bad.[20] Ironically they have just increased the likelihood of relationship failure, not protected themselves from it.

> ### Sliding Without Deciding
>
> "He and his daughter would come over and watch movies. It just got easier for them to spend the night. Then they started coming over and never left. Pretty soon, they moved in all their stuff."

Essentially, cohabitation is choosing second best and then wondering why it didn't work out for the best. Instead, choose God's best for you. Date with intentionality, separate and apart from the confusion of sex and cohabitation, and your dating decisions will have much more clarity and integrity for both you and the kids.

An Imbalanced Dance of Want

What happens when one person's green light intersects with the other person's yellow or red light? You have what I like to call the dance of want.

In a general sense, the dance is about who wants whom, and how much each wants the other. The dance occurs throughout dating. The first time is during the pre-dating phase. For example, when you have feelings for someone but don't know if they are also interested in you, you aren't sure whether to step toward them or away . . . and when.

Even after a first—or many—dates this dynamic continues. One person may find themselves wishing for more time together or daydreaming of the other and then wondering if the other is equally interested in them. No one wants to want more than they are wanted. (Do you hear the fear in that statement?) Before asking a woman to marry him, a man wonders, *What if she says no or not now?* Even after marriage the dance continues as the ebb and flow of life leaves partners wondering, *Why hasn't she spoken to me as much lately?* or *Why is it that I initiate sex most of the time?*

The dating dance cannot be helped. Until you solidify your commitment to each other in marriage, you cannot help but wonder if the other is as invested in you—and the developing "us"—as you are. By the way, if in your first marriage you found yourself repeatedly wanting your spouse to want you more, you may be hypersensitive to being the more motivated partner in a new dating relationship. Manage this ghost and your fear reactions or you may push away someone who is still working through their feelings for you. Some people play the want game, pretending not to really love the other person as much as they do to see if the other fights for the relationship (i.e., playing hard to get). But that just perpetuates a dance of want that is unstable and manipulative.

Instead, proactively define the relationship from your point of view and be authentic with your feelings. Is that risky? Yes, it is. And it's also how you determine if you have a mutually supported relationship or a one-sided one.

But what if you've been authentic and patient and the other is still not moving toward you? What if you have a clear green light and the other person has a persistent cautious yellow, and you continue the relationship? Typically what crystallizes is a pursue-distance dynamic that becomes, in and of itself, a serious red light.

If you find yourself chasing someone who is repeatedly unwilling to pursue you, stop being willing to settle for the crumbs they toss for you on the floor. For years Debbie dated a guy who loved her but wouldn't marry her (though he would live with her) because she had, in his words, "undisciplined" children. Debbie admitted that she was a poor parent and that her kids had behavior problems. She tried to improve, but every time she recommitted herself to better parenting, she gave in to the kids and her boyfriend backed a little further away from marriage. Debbie sent me an email summarizing the situation. In parentheses you can see what I was thinking as I read it.

"He isn't sure he wants to continue dating me." (To be more precise, he is interested in you—and sex—but not in partnering with your undisciplined parenting. He doesn't want the package, but you're willing to settle for what you can get.) "I'm trying everything I can to not let him give up on me." (Oh, Debbie, no one has enough want for two people.) "I know that I love him and want to spend my life with him, but he is reluctant to put forth any effort at all toward me." (Please wake up and smell the coffee. Stop chasing a squirrel thinking it wants to be caught.) "I just don't know what else to do." (I've got a suggestion: Recognize the red light in front of you, let go, and move on. By the way, this means having to deal with your fear of being alone.)

There are many reasons people like Debbie are willing to settle for crumbs of want from a partner: a history of one-sided relationships makes another feel familiar; they fear getting old alone or having their biological clock stop ticking; and they don't think they are valuable enough to be loved well. On the other hand, there are many reasons some dating partners remain guarded: the

> **Motivation and Relationship Influence**
>
> - The person least invested in a relationship has the most power (influence).
> - When pursuing an elusive partner, the highly invested partner feels frustrated and insecure.

fear of being hurt, being unsure of relationship "fit"; wanting to wait till a new season of their life arrives (i.e., after graduation, promotion, accumulated wealth, etc.); or, as in the case of Debbie's boyfriend, not wanting to marry the entire blended family package. Actually, I see this a lot. Sometimes one partner (usually the biological parent) is less concerned about how the blended family will fare and they get into a dance of want with the would-be stepparent ("I'm going to talk you into not being afraid of us").

If you find yourself stuck in this dynamic—for whatever the reason—step back and recognize that the pursue-distance dance has created a fragile and emotionally unstable situation for everyone involved. Then, stop wanting for two. Let go of trying to motivate the other person to invest more, give more, and want more. If they resolve their concerns and find a new level of investment, congratulations, you've got a fair chance at a healthy relationship. If they don't, let them go.

Having an "Affair" With the Person They Almost Are

This red light is for those of you who have been dating for a while and are stuck. You have a love-hate relationship with the person but can't get any clarity on what's going on.

In my opinion, one of the most pathetic lines in a romantic movie (*Jerry Maguire*) is when Dorothy Boyd, played by actress Renee Zellweger, tells her sister that she is in love with Jerry, played by Tom Cruise, even though he is distant, uncommitted, and inattentive. "I love him for the man he almost is." That means she's having an affair with the fantasy of the man, not the man himself.

One man I counseled had been dating a woman for three years. He described their recurring on-and-off dynamic as him breaking up with her because she was harsh and critical, only to take her back because he missed her few good qualities and mostly the potential he saw in her and in their relationship. Plus, to get him to take her back, she repeatedly promised to act nicer.

After a brief "honeymoon" she would again go back to being the same mean person; after pleading with her to change, he would break up with her again. In the meantime, she was bonding with his child, which added to his sense of obligation to stay with her. Ever optimistic, he would again put up with who she was while dreaming about who she almost was. After three years, he felt stuck. He wasn't. He just needed to stop having an affair with who she promised to be and break up with who she really was.

Why would someone focus on the fantasy person instead of the real person? I've seen many singles who felt like this was their last chance at marriage and they just couldn't give it up. Others see their children bonding with the other person and/or their children and fear hurting their kids, so they hold themselves hostage to what they think their kids need. And others discount their concerns by determining that they are being too judgmental. Whatever the reason, if you are stuck in this rut, you really aren't stuck.

GREEN LIGHT

The absence of serious yellow lights and red lights is a green light for proceeding with a relationship. But ultimately the decision to marry needs more than that. You need a sense of direction, purpose, and safety in the relationship, and you need time to confirm your couple and family fit. Your confidence about choosing marriage will also increase dramatically when children, friends, family, and God's Spirit confirm your "us-ness."

Do you still have a green light? The next few chapters will walk you further down the road.

Discussion Questions

1. Case Study: Do you remember Paul and Brenda's advice to their dating friends? Don't rush into marriage; make sure you are ready to marry the entire package that comes along with the person you have fallen in love with, or don't marry. Read the following scenario and discuss it together.

Dear Smart Stepfamilies,

I am a single woman with no children and am dating a man who has never been married but has three children (two with one woman and one with another). At first I ran from the idea of dating him, but we became great friends and, after a few years of friendship, I gave dating a try. But now I am confused.

We don't seem to get much time together in part because his children don't live with him and he feels he must jump through hoops to appease their mothers in order to get time with them. Most days he tries to spend time after school with them and then put them to bed. Then he wants to spend time with me after that (which is usually after 10:00 p.m.). On weekends he would be "on call" just in case the mothers decided they would allow him to see the children. As you can imagine, we seldom get to keep our date plans. Sometimes he would visit me late at night, and that just set us up for sexual situations that were displeasing to God.

I care for this man and think we might be good together, but I'm troubled by what is happening. What should I do?

- How would you respond to this woman? Explain your reasoning and discuss the dynamics at play here.

- How would you respond if talking with the boyfriend/father?

2. Flip back through the chapter and review the yellow lights. Which are flashing in your dating relationship (past or present)? Rate their significance from 1 to 10 with 10 being the most menacing.

3. Now review the red lights. Which are turned on? In what ways are you tempted to minimize them?

4. List any other yellow or red lights you can think of that were not mentioned in this chapter.

Chapter 8

Going Deeper

Once we got really serious, my boyfriend and I took a five-week parenting class together, attended a one-day remarriage seminar, and completed a ten-week financial course together. It really helped us evaluate our future.

Amanda

So far, all the lights are green. Now what do you do? How do you move past "I love you" to "I'm confident I want to spend the rest of my life with you"?

Amanda, quoted above, and her boyfriend are on to something. They intentionally engaged themselves in structured classes and activities that fostered constructive dialogue. After dating for a while, some couples allow their dating process to wander aimlessly. Brittney shared, "I was in a relationship that I thought had potential for marriage, but then we got in an unhealthy rut. No growth toward God, just the ho-hum of 'How's your day?' After a year of going nowhere, I expressed my need for more but got no serious response from him. I had to make a decision to move on."

Intentionally inserting structures, like attending seminars or reading a book together, helps to deepen a relationship. In Brittney's case, it helped reveal that her level of want was greater than her boyfriend's. This chapter will provide structures you can put in place and topics to discuss to deepen your relationship. But before we proceed, now that you're serious, it's important to remind yourself where you're going.

ENGAGED TO A SAVIOR

In Matthew 22 there is an interesting dilemma presented to Jesus; his response is one you'll never hear shared during a wedding. The Sadducees present a case study to Jesus about a woman who had been married and widowed seven times. "At the resurrection," they asked, "whose wife will she be of the seven, since all of them were married to her?" (Matthew 22:28). Before hearing Jesus' reply, let's push Pause for a moment. Imagine how Hollywood or your favorite romance novelist would answer. "Well, the one she loved the most, of course," they might reply. Or perhaps, "Only her true soul mate could spend eternity with her in heaven; otherwise it wouldn't be heaven!" If you were asked that question, what would your answer be?

Now push Play to hear Jesus' reply. "You are in error because you do not know the Scriptures or the power of God. At the resurrection people will neither marry nor be given in marriage; they will be like the angels in heaven" (Matthew 22:29–30).

What? There's no marriage in heaven? But I thought (didn't you, too?) that eternity with the one you love would be the ultimate ending to true romance. Well, it is—but not in the way we assume.

The Bible begins and ends with a wedding. In the beginning, because of the aloneness of man, God gives the first bride away, and on the last day when Christ comes back for his bride, the church, we will all be joined with him in heaven in perfect oneness.

In light of that truth I guess you could say we're all engaged to our Savior. And when he comes, implies Jesus' response, we won't need marriage to fill our aloneness because the power and presence of God will fulfill our every longing. We will experience ultimate oneness with the One who created us and live happily ever after.

Do you remember being in kindergarten and going on a field trip? The teacher probably paired you up with a friend and told you to hold hands and stick together. Or the teacher might have grouped a few students together with a chaperone so no one got lost. God has pretty much done the same thing for us.

We are on the field trip of life and we've left the safety of the classroom, but we haven't arrived at the destination yet. When Jesus comes, we will have arrived, but until then, we're still vulnerable. To help us not get lost, he's created two groups to help us find our way. First, we've been put into a small group of people called the church. Here we look after one another and encourage one another as we see the day approaching (Hebrews 10:25). This is a place for singles as well as couples and families. Others of us find a buddy—a spiritual traveling buddy—to whom we are accountable. We help each other stay on the path and together strive to bring our children along with us on the journey to the ultimate destination.

> "Before I date someone seriously, I need to see the fruit of the Spirit in them and I need to know that they accept me for who I am but love me enough to encourage my growth with Christ so I will become more like him."—Brittney

Marriage to a person is not our ultimate destination; being wed to our Lord is. Single people need that perspective so they won't overvalue getting married, and married people need that perspective so they won't lose sight of their purpose in being together.[1] And dating people need that perspective so that they will date with the purpose of finding someone who can become their buddy during the field trip of life and ultimately usher them to the arms of their Savior.

Going deeper for any purpose other than this is a waste of time and could become an idol that detours your walk toward Christ. On the other hand, going deep in the spiritual disciplines, for example, will lead you toward Christ and have the added benefit of solidifying your hearts and empowering a healthy marriage. Therefore, make shared godliness a priority for your relationship (and if the other person is unable to join you there, consider that a yellow—and some would say red—light).

Pray Together

You can learn so much about a person just by listening to them pray. What do they pray about? For example, are they the center of their prayers or do they have a heart for the poor, underprivileged, and broken? What concerns them or fills their thoughts? How do they approach the Father—with legalistic fear or humble confidence in God's grace? If they can't pray openly with you, you take the lead and see if they can't eventually get there. Many people find prayer an intimate activity (far more so than sex) that is intimidating. That should show us just how powerful it is—and how helpful it is to a relationship.

Knowing Yourself

Most people find praying with a romantic partner or spouse difficult. What makes you anxious about it? Write down your feelings and fears.

Study the Scriptures

Try to engage one another in learning from God's Word, whether in a Bible study or small group with others, with your children, or just by yourselves. Talk about what God is teaching you and discuss how to live it out. And if you really want to go deep, share your temptations and confess sin to each other. A relationship that offers both accountability and encouragement about such things is one that can reach the destination.

Serve Beside Each Other

Turn your shared faith into shared service; get outside of yourself and help someone else in the name of Christ. This is primarily an act of love for those God loves, and yet it also feeds and informs your dating.

DEFINE THE RELATIONSHIP

Before I share many other practical strategies for deepening your relationship and informing your decisions about marriage, remember to again openly define the relationship. As I shared earlier, couples should overtly discuss the status of their relationship at every phase. Before adding intentional structures to deepen your relationship, it would be advisable to have the "I'm ready for us to be very intentional" conversation. Assuming both of you agree that your level of want is moving you toward marriage, then implementation of the strategies in this chapter will be easy. If only one of you is ready to define the relationship as serious, then you'll need to slow down. Either way, at least you'll both know where you stand.

If both of you are seeking to deepen the relationship, it's wise to share this with your children. They, too, need to know the status of your relationship. This can be accomplished with another "What if?" conversation. What if Jeremy and I were getting serious? What if we all started spending a lot more time together? What if I were to take his daughter out for lunch someday—how would you feel about that?

Each answer gives you information about how the kids are feeling and what their concerns might be. You might also discover that they already suspected you were serious (our kids can read us pretty well), but still, the conversation lets everyone know of your intentions. It also invites them to go with you to the next phase of coupleness and familyness.

GOING DEEPER STRATEGIES

The following steps are not in any particular order, and not all of them will make sense for your relationship. Feel free to implement the ideas that make sense at this point in your relationship. If you've already found your way to doing some of these, you're on the right track.

Explore Your "Fit" and Relationship Health

Throughout the book I have mentioned the online Couple Checkup inventory. Used by individual couples throughout the world and churches, the inventory is backed by thirty-five years of research and has been taken by millions of couples. The Couple Checkup is an assessment tool designed to identify the unique strengths and growth areas of your relationship. And because it tailors itself to your relationship type, you can take it at each season, whether dating, engaged, or married, in order to assess your strengths and where you need to grow if you are going to have a vibrant marriage.

Immediately after completing the assessment, couples receive a ten-page Couple Checkup Report assessing over twenty aspects of couple relationships, including expectations, communication, managing conflict, finances, affection and sexuality, spiritual beliefs, and dating issues (or if engaged, a scale that deals with marital preparation). You also receive an extensive discussion guide designed to help you learn proven relationship skills in these and other areas. Research has shown that this process improves relationships by stimulating honest dialogue, increasing understanding, and empowering couples.

In addition, couples who want to prepare specifically for the challenges of remarriage will want to get *The Remarriage Checkup,* the book written by the innovator of the Checkup, Dr. David Olson, and me. In that book we report on our research of what predicts healthy remarriages, and we walk couples through a process of using their couple report to enhance their relationship stability and trust.

Taking the Couple Checkup has two distinct advantages. First, it provides you and your partner an objective X ray of your relationship health. Lots of couples marry with a false confidence in the quality of their relationship; the fog of love or infatuation distorts their discernment, and they make decisions based on subjective feelings.

The Couple Checkup is not a pass/fail assessment, that is, it's not a compatibility test and it's not going to recommend whether you stay together or get married. That is for you to decide. But when taken by both partners it will clearly identify whether you have a strong relationship, a moderate one, or a fragile one. This creates the second advantage for dating couples. Learning about your weaknesses helps you as a couple target specific ways to improve. No more shooting in the dark. No more wondering what you need to talk about before deciding on marriage. The report will tell you what you need to discuss and what needs to improve, and the book *The Remarriage Checkup* (and small group discussion guide) will tell you how to do it.

> **Take the Couple Checkup**
>
> Get one free Individual Report at www.smart stepfamilies.com by using the voucher code provided inside the back cover of this book. This code also provides a 50 percent discount if you upgrade to the full couple report (available after you have completed your free Individual Profile).

There is one limitation, however, to the Checkup. It is a couple relationship profile, not a family profile. It will help you know whether you are on the same page about stepparenting, but it won't assess the joys or fears of your children. It won't let you know whether your ex is going to make your life miserable and it won't predict how kids will receive a stepparent's authority. You still have to attend to the familyness issues yourself.

Date the Kids

If you are the single parent, perhaps you have been a bit protective of your kids up to this point. Single parents often have legitimate concerns about exposing their children to would-be child molesters or a child bonding with someone only to have them step out of the child's life after a breakup. Those are reasonable concerns, but now that you are actively trying to deepen your relationship, it's time to start deepening the potential steprelationships, as well. This includes "dating" the other's children and letting the children spend time together. Frequently this is already happening to a degree. But what I'm talking about is proactive, intentional "family dating."

If You Don't Have Kids

Be sure your dating partner is in agreement that it's time for you to become more intentional with their kids. Discuss what this might look like and what strategies you'll use. If you have been ready for this for some time but the parent is not, ask what their fears or concerns might be and hear their heart. Agree on small steps you can take to help lessen their fears and connect with the kids.

Kelsey and her fiancé shared their family dating best practice: "We have weekly meals together and we plan at least one event a month that is required attendance for all the children. We have also planned several weekend trips together." This type of activity is on target for this phase of your dating. Essentially, time together is what fosters connection and a growing sense of family, which will, in turn, increase your confidence in a decision to marry. If the structured time backfires and kids get annoyed by it, back up a step and don't force it down their throats. Closeness has to be chosen and can't be forced upon them.

Likewise, when a dating partner dates a kid by spending focused time with them with or without the parent, they should gauge the child's level of openness and mirror it. Some children are just waiting for you to walk into their world, and they gladly invite you in. Others will avoid a one-on-one outing like the plague. Try to meet them where they are and grow from there. It helps if you engage them around things they are already interested in. Study their preferences, desires, and wounds and try to enter each as allowed. Your basic goal as the outsider is to get to know them and build a basic level of respect and trust. Love may or may not occur; for now, just connect.

Mary, a single mom of two teenagers, offered some good insight when she suggested that couples in this period of dating include the kids in as many decisions as possible. Teens in particular need to feel some power over their lives, and bringing them into decisions is a good way to do that—and it shows them some respect. That, in turn, helps them have respect for your relationship.

Having some control in choices and the direction of the family is very much related to past losses. In an earlier chapter I suggested that for both adults and children, the deepening of a new relationship and the sense that marriage is approaching heightens both fear and sadness. Don't be surprised if kids start talking about their deceased parent more as they sense you getting more serious. Or perhaps they'll make sure that your boyfriend, for example, knows that their loyalty is to their biological dad and not him. These stake-in-the-ground statements feel needed when a child is feeling guilty over what is happening. Be sure to listen and affirm these emotions (see the next section), not dismiss or argue with them. Doing so only builds a wall to your relationship. Jerry told our ministry this is exactly why he went to family therapy with his kids. They needed a place to talk about their mother's death and at the same time discuss their feelings about his girlfriend, Sonia. Giving his kids a trusted guide to help them sort through some things was wise.

Kids Talk

- Don't try to impress me; I can see through phony.
- Don't try to replace my dad/mom, and don't act like you're my parent—you're not.
- Don't smother me; I'll let you in when I'm good and ready.
- No PDA (public displays of affection)—it's kind of gross.
- I like you—sometimes I think I love you—and I feel weird, guilty, and scared when I do.

Learn to Tune In and Turn Toward

Listening with empathy is an amazing skill in interpersonal relationships. Whether to a co-worker, friend, family member, or spouse, listening with the intent of seeing the world through the eyes of another facilitates emotional safety between the two parties and fosters shared understanding. This in turn invites each to share with more transparency. When this is understood and validated, both experience greater intimacy with each other.

> ### Part-time Kids
>
> Two challenges:
> 1. Having infrequent time with them makes bonding harder.
> 2. When they do visit, try to balance their need for one-on-one time with their parent and the couple's need for family dating.

There are some subtle but very important skills that people can develop to help them be more empathetic. They have been described as tuning in and turning toward your partner.[2] Partners who tune in are aware of what is going on in the inner world of the other and they attend to it. "I know you've been worried about your son lately. How did it go with Dylan today?" This invites a sharing of inner worlds and says, "I'm here for you."

Turning toward the other, particularly when they are experiencing a negative emotion, requires a tolerance for anxiety, especially if the emotion is about you. Having this skill starts with believing that negative emotions aren't bad, but are instead a normal part of life. People with a low tolerance for negativity try to squelch it as soon as possible. Have you ever tried to talk someone out of a negative feeling (especially one about you)? It doesn't work—and it pushes them further away from you. Rather, enter the person's world, turn toward them, to explore and understand the emotion. "It's obvious you are feeling hurt. Help me understand."

Now here's what true masters are able to do: They listen beneath the other's words to hear the desire embedded deep within. Their words may be "Yeah, I'm hurt. We make plans to be together and then you break them at the drop of a hat to accommodate your kids' every beck and call." A dismissing person will reply, "Now wait a minute. You know my kids are important to me. Don't get between me and my kids." With a message of "you can't feel that way," this argument is off to the races (and both people are going to feel more distant and less safe as a result). Rather, listen beneath the words to hear the desire, the request therein. What they really said was, "I'm missing you." A master listener will turn toward that desire and validate the feeling (even if they don't understand it). "What you're telling me is that you enjoy being with me and feel disappointed when something interrupts our time together." When hearts connect around desire, then and only then can the couple have a nondefensive, safe conversation about the delicacies of balancing their couple time with the needs of the children. Highly respected marital researcher John Gottman said, "There is a longing or a wish,

When the Kid Is an Adult

Strive to have peer-to-peer turning toward conversations, not parent-child ones. This shows respect to the adult child and invites respect.

and therefore a recipe, within every negative emotion."[3] Can you find the longing . . . and follow the recipe? A master partner and companion can.

Now here's the bonus. People who have the skills to tune in to emotion make better stepparents because they are not afraid of the emotions of children. In particular, they know what to do with negative emotions. For example, a stepmother with this skill is not dismissive of a child who displays sadness around Mother's Day because they aren't with their mother. Instead, she turns toward the child, acknowledges and labels the sadness (and pain), and invites the child to share it with her. A dismissive stepmother would feel personally attacked in this situation and get lost in how it made her feel instead of focusing on the child; she may even try to talk the child into feeling better (a strategy that never works). Again, a stepparent with a tolerance for negative emotions would be compassionate, patient with the child, and view the situation as an opportunity to help coach the child (learn more about emotional coaching in *The Smart Stepmom* and *The Smart Stepdad*). Just as in a couple's relationship, this response fosters emotional safety and a movement toward one another; it invites stepchildren to draw toward a stepparent. This in turn is a homerun for the family as a whole.

TOPICS TO DISCUSS—REALLY DISCUSS

The Remarriage Checkup book and online Couple Checkup assessment and report will spur dialogue around a number of important topics related to your couple relationship. Topics like money management, how you expect to manage conflict (i.e., the rules for fighting fair), personal habits that concern you, and your expectations for sex in marriage need focused conversation and agreement should you decide to move forward together. Money management, for example, is not just about "Are you a spender or a saver?" or "Should we compile all our assets or keep them separate after we marry?" It is also about your values and your understanding of stewardship from a biblical standpoint. These conversations are vital to deepening your relationship.

> **Financial Conversations**
>
> A list of money questions for dating couples to discuss is available at smartstepfamilies.com/view/money-questions.

Another critical topic to discuss is parenting. As you read that, you're probably thinking, *Well, duh. Of course that's important—there are kids to raise (or if adults, to mentor or support).* But apparently that isn't as clear to most single parents as you'd think. Only about one-third of moms discuss with their dating partner before marriage some aspect of his future role as stepfather to her children (e.g., his behavior and affection toward the children, his role in child care, or discipline and behavioral management), and 19 percent never discuss anything![4] If you ask me, that's evidence of big assumptions such as "He's a great guy, he will be a great father" and "Because we get along so well, we will see eye to eye on parenting." Such assumptions are extremely risky.

Likewise, I've noticed that many singles without children of their own have a strong hesitation to bring up parenting matters with their dating partner because they think *I don't have kids, what do I know about parenting?* Others fear that it will appear as if they are being critical of the kids. So in an attempt not to create conflict, they just avoid the subject altogether. Bottom line: The couple does not process parenting styles, strategies, their knowledge of child development, or their preferences in discipline.

What's at stake here is the children's adjustment to the new family and the stepparent. Family conflict that begins with parenting issues quickly transitions to marital ones. As I shared earlier in the book, couple satisfaction before marriage is centered on the couple's relationship, but after the wedding is increasingly tied to parental unity or conflict (as well as other third-party stressors like difficult ex-spouses). Being a couple and being unified parents are two different things; do not assume you will be a good team just because you love each other. It's critical to thoroughly discuss:

> **Once Serious With Someone, What Should You Talk About?**
>
> Judy recommended couples discuss their parenting expectations, how to discipline, and daily routines, including everything from how to get kids up in the morning, to bath time and bedtime routines, to what you do on the weekends and family traditions on holidays.

- your expectations of the children's chores and responsibilities;
- behavioral management of the children;
- the role of punishment in your home and which strategies you will and won't utilize;

- how you will train the children spiritually;
- whether you will have more children;
- the influence of co-parents on your household, the boundaries you will attempt to put in place, and how to manage stressors that arise from the other home; and
- how you will function as a parent-stepparent team, including how to capitalize on your relational strengths with the children, who will impose discipline and under what conditions, and coming to an understanding of the limitations of the stepparent's role and influence.

The details of these matters are beyond the scope of this book, but all of these topics are specifically addressed in my books *The Smart Stepdad* and *The Smart Stepmom* (coauthored with Laura Petherbridge). In addition, each book contains two chapters for the biological parent detailing their unique and critical role in setting the stepparent up for success. I strongly recommend that you read one or, if appropriate, both of those books, discuss the concepts, and agree on which will govern your parenting should you marry. I can't tell you how many people have read those books well into their marriage and reported to me, "We have made so many mistakes and now I understand what we did wrong. I wish I would have read this before we married."

Find a Mentor and Learn All You Can About Stepfamily Living

Nearly twenty years of counseling, coaching, and training blended families has revealed a secret of successful blended family couples: They work harder at getting smarter about stepfamily living. Getting smarter means learning all you can about how stepfamilies function and operate best, and why they have the unique complexities that they do. You may know how to drive a car, but driving in snow and icy conditions requires a different knowledge and skill set. Nearly all blended families have inclement weather to manage as they drive, so adopt the attitude of a learner.

To do this you can read the books I've recommended or visit smartstepfamilies .com (with the largest bank of articles on stepfamily living available). But let me also recommend that you find a mentor couple to walk with you through your dating, decisions about marriage, and first two years after the wedding. Look for a couple who

When a Parent Is Deceased

Stepparents should explore what type of parent they were. Don't try to replicate them (be yourself), but realize that who they were creates expectations in the children.

has been married at least ten years, take them to lunch, and ask them if they'd be willing to walk beside you. They don't have to have all the answers—perhaps you could read *The Smart Stepfamily* or watch my *Remarriage Success* DVD together and let the content ignite insightful conversations—they just have to be willing to share some of their perspective.

One indirect way of being mentored is sitting in on your church's class or small group for blended family couples. (If they don't have one, ask them to begin one soon!) Listen to the couples discuss real-life matters and glean from their experience what is helpful and what isn't. You will never regret the effort it takes to get smart.

Discussion Questions

1. How might an intentional family outing reveal the need to slow your dating?

2. So far, how have you been intentional to foster depth in your dating? What other ideas has this chapter generated for you?

3. What is unsettling about Jesus' teaching that there is no marriage in heaven (Matthew 22:28–30)?

4. How does it recalibrate your image of marriage to think of it as God's spiritual buddy system meant to usher us toward the ultimate destination and "marriage" to Christ?

5. How often have you prayed together and under what circumstances? Most couples find praying together without others present very difficult. The level of insecurity and anxiety in doing so is a testimony to how intimate it is. Discuss together how you can begin praying together more often.

6. Without discussing it first, each of you should write a brief paragraph defining your relationship as you currently understand it. Then share and discuss what you've written.

7. Review the sidebar Kids Talk (p. 171). What do you think your kids are thinking about your relationship?

8. Rate your ability to tune in and turn toward negative emotions on a scale of 1 to 10 (with 10 being the most ideal). What rating would your partner give you? What rating would the children give you?

9. Discuss if and when you will take the online Couple Checkup. Once you have, use your Couple Report to stimulate conversation about your strengths and growth areas.

10. Discerning your fit as a parenting team is critical. What books, classes, or seminars could you access to help you explore and develop a parenting plan?

11. List the names of five potential mentor couples. Decide if and when you will approach them for guidance.

Marital Commitment and Stepfamily Preparation

At this point you're pretty sure you've caught the fish of your dreams. But how do you know for certain? And once you make the commitment to pull them into your boat, how do you tell the kids and prepare yourselves to become a new family?

This section will explore these and other important questions and help you build confidence in your future.

Chapter 9

Re-Engage? Decisions About Marriage

Our wedding is planned for later this year, but I plan to post-pone it. I love him and the children, but it is so hard.

Facebook Submission

I think it's getting harder in our culture today for people to pull the trigger on a covenant commitment to another person. The collective anxiety in our world about the instability of marriage screams—via TV, movies, online media, and social networking sites—"Don't do it." And people are listening. Cohabitation has risen dramatically before a first marriage, which doesn't usually happen until people are in their late twenties and already have a child. In mid-life, cohabitation between marriages is exceedingly common, and more and more later-life couples are choosing cohabitation instead of trying to merge retirement plans and three generations of family relationships. We lack confidence in "happily ever after" and, therefore, keep trying to find ways of being with someone without having to fully be with someone. And yet God has clearly created marriage for our provision and protection.

"Fine," you say, "but that doesn't help me know whether to marry *this* person or whether the kid-adult combinations will work out."

One woman posted the following to an online forum. She was already engaged but far from pulling the trigger:

> *My fiancé and I are getting married in several months. I have three children and he has two. We began dating a couple years ago; before that I had not seriously dated anyone for eight years because I chose to focus on my children and only date someone that I would consider marrying someday. We fell in love, and at times I feel like we can work through the obstacles of blending our families, but at other times I feel hopeless. I am not sure if I am just getting cold feet or if we have major issues.*
>
> *My children have no father in their life; his kids live with their mother and they visit us whenever they like. He has been more than a father to my children and they absolutely LOVE him. He takes off work to go to their school events and much more. They have never had a father and they don't take him for granted.*
>
> *We broke up once because I didn't think I could do it. He spends money trying to keep up with his ex's new husband; I'm afraid of losing everything I have worked for if we get married. After we broke up, one of his kids stayed in touch with me and begged us to get back together. She said that with me and her father together, she actually felt like she was part of a family. She was so excited when we became engaged, but sometimes it feels like she doesn't like me at all. I'm confused.*

DECISION POINTS

"So how do we know if we should get married?"

That is a question I hear often. Even after dating well and giving careful consideration to all of the dynamics involved, the answer isn't easy. There are a plethora of matters that people evaluate as they consider engagement: their life stage, financial situation, the openness of the children, how much they desire a life partner, the quality of the relationship and perceived future together, how much they love the other person, the level of conflict in the relationship—on and on the list goes. I've talked about a number of these throughout the book, but only you can know what all these factors are for you, and only you can evaluate the pros and cons, risks and rewards of each in order to make a decision. Some of these matters weigh more heavily than others, and since you determine how much they weigh, ultimately you determine which impact your decision most. Some matters are potential deal breakers; others give cause for continued dating while delaying a decision.

> Catching couples in the throes of the "integration years" (see chapter 10) will likely find them under stress. Talk to blended families who have been married ten years or longer to balance your hesitations and hear about the long-term rewards of healthy blended families.

May I suggest that it is unrealistic to expect that you can do away with every concern or anxiety related to this decision. What you are looking for in general is:

- confidence in your relationship
- conviction that you are willing to give your life away in the loving service of the other (and their children)
- trust that your partner is willing to do the same for you
- an educated, objective sense (as opposed to a love-intoxicated delusional sense) that the children are reasonably open to your union and a new family, and that their emotional, psychological, and spiritual health will be well served by your marriage

Confidence

Joshua sent me an email explaining his decision hesitations:

I know you don't remember me, but we talked on the phone a couple of months ago and I ordered one of your books and a video. My girlfriend and I were thinking of getting married and blending our families. We wanted to do it the right way and were in no hurry, so we did some research and found your ministry.

We both watched your video, read The Smart Stepfamily together, and took your advice suggesting we find a blended family to talk to. What we found is probably not what most would expect and certainly not what we expected. We couldn't find a stepfamily that really thrived—not one that looked like ours, anyway. All of the families we looked at were just surviving, having a multitude of issues surrounding the children; some were on divorce's doorstep again. This scared us to death. It seems to us that the blended family is a good idea for adults, but not so good for the kids.

> "I am a single female . . . never been married. I am engaged to a man with two children, ages nine and seven. Our wedding is planned for later this year, but I plan to postpone it. I love him and the children, but it is so hard. All he thinks about is his kids— but isn't that the way it is supposed to be? I feel so selfish because I think *What about me?* I feel guilty and unsure of what to do. Is there anyone who can help me—and us—decide what to do?"

To their credit, Joshua and his girlfriend were proactively learning all they could about stepfamily living, but the feedback they got from those living the realities was causing hesitation. In short, their confidence was low.

I've suggested throughout this book that the quality of the future stepparent-stepchildren relationship(s) is just as important to a marriage decision as the quality of the couple relationship. You need confidence in both to move forward.

If you are lacking confidence, give full consideration as to why, and don't get engaged until your confidence rises. One predictable trap for people who lack full confidence before making a decision to marry is that after the wedding, when the inevitable conflicts and disappointments of blended living occur, they look back on the decision and label it a bad one. Recasting the past in light of a stressful present is highly predictive of marital disillusionment and divorce[1] because it closes you off to seeing the relationship as a good one or one worthy of hard work. Ignoring your own hesitancies before marriage is a setup for trouble later. When your confidence is high, make a decision for marriage; until then, keep seeking to resolve the concerns or gracefully bow out of the relationship if you can't.

Commitment and Trust

Let me remind you of something you already know. Marriage is tough. Not because it's inherently difficult, but because marriage reveals our selfishness. Therefore, it forces us, if we want to experience trust and intimacy, to do the hard work of confronting and sacrificing our selfishness. Marriage is tough because intimacy always requires more of us than we expected. (By the way, this is one significant way God grows us up into the likeness of our Savior.)

To help us stay engaged in this painful process of growing up, God in his infinite wisdom asks each person to make a covenant that binds them together throughout life. Without this permanence, most people won't subject themselves to the process of maturation and discipleship that marriage brings; instead they wiggle out when the going gets tough. The "till death do us part" promise helps to constrain our momentary unwillingness to mature and strengthens our motivation to persist, grow, and learn to love.

What I'm suggesting to you is that commitment in the form of marital vows expressed at a wedding is a significant turning point for any relationship because it helps foster a living out of the commitment. It builds a wall of motivation around the marriage that helps each person to allow God to grow them into the person the marriage and blended family needs them to be. Waiting for a guarantee that this is the right person doesn't take into consideration who they will be after making a commitment—or for that matter, who you will be. Instead, evaluate whether you and your dating partner have the resolve and determination to live out a covenant commitment. If not, slow down or back up a step. But if you do trust the level of resolve in both of you, keep moving forward.

What should you do if one of you is ready to make that commitment and the other is not?

This brings us back to the dance of want that I discussed in chapter 7. If one of you is feeling God's blessing on the relationship and is ready to move forward, great. But don't use that desire as a hammer to make the other want the relationship just as much. Instead, make space for them to reach their own decision in their own timing.

"But what if they aren't moving fast enough?" someone might ask. Well, one thing's for sure—saying, "Hurry up and want!" won't help. Rather, take this approach:

- Patiently continue dating. Date within the level of closeness and commitment—the comfort zone, if you will—of the other; be intentional to deepen your understanding of each other and your circumstances.

- Wrestle with your impatience. Usually there is fear underneath that needs to be attended to. Name the fear and process it with someone other than your dating partner (that puts undue pressure on them to alleviate your fear for you, which fosters a guilt that is not conducive to them making an unencumbered decision for the relationship).

- Identify together any specific concerns about your couple or family relationships. Seek solutions when you can identify them. Realize there may be some concerns that do not have a resolution within your control (e.g., concerns about the negativity of an ex-spouse or when you have been married before and the other can't get comfortable with not being your "one and only").

- Give time for the hesitant person to find resolution to their concerns. Remember, time is a friend to your us-ness.

- At some point, however, the higher desire person will grow weary of waiting. Only they will know when they can't wait any longer and need to move on. Feel free to let the other know when you're growing weary (define the relationship), but don't threaten a breakup just to get them to want more.

• If you are unable to find mutual direction for the future, courageously end the relationship.

Mike and Charlene pulled me aside at a conference. They had read a couple of my books and were attending a conference, but they had a dilemma that needed personal attention.

Mike had been divorced about sixteen years. He had raised his three girls and now they were young professionals living on their own. While raising them, he dated a few people but focused primarily on his children.

Charlene was about fourteen years younger than Mike and was busy raising her two children: Tommy, age twelve, and Katy, age ten. Mike and Charlene had been dating for about two years when it occurred to both of them that they were stuck when it came to a decision about marriage.

I must tell you, most couples that pull me aside at a conference and ask whether they are ready to marry have not done their homework. Unlike you, who have been reading this book, they haven't studied about stepfamily living, nor have they considered the spiritual implications of such a decision. In addition, they are typically having sex and in a hurry to tie the knot. None of this was true for Mike and Charlene. They had successfully managed their sexual temptations, had sought outside counsel and wisdom about the tasks of becoming a stepfamily, were being very patient with the dating process, and were very much in love with each other. So what was the problem?

The closer they got to marriage, the more Mike realized he didn't have any desire to raise more children. Charlene's kids were about to enter adolescence, and he knew how much emotional energy that would require of him; he just didn't want to be responsible for them or to them. He felt very bad about this. His first question to me was "Is there something wrong with me? Am I just being selfish?"

"Selfish would be marrying her under false pretenses and then disengaging from the kids," I said. As we talked through his feelings, it became clear to me that Mike was not a self-absorbed man. He just didn't want more kids, and he knew that if he married Charlene he couldn't go halfway in parenting. It was an all-or-nothing decision. I agreed.

I was impressed with Mike's self-awareness and honesty with Charlene. They had discussed this numerous times, and again the conversation led him to admit that it wouldn't be right to ask Charlene to keep waiting for him. This maturity impressed me.

But Charlene's maturity throughout the conversation impressed me even more. She was the higher desire partner who had been waiting on Mike. She had been hopeful about a future with him— and even now still was. I'm sure the weight of his decision would not settle in until they really stopped seeing each other, but she took the hard news well. She could have responded out of her emotions—fear, rejection, disappointment—but instead she responded out of wisdom. As much as she wanted Mike in her life, she knew it wouldn't be wise to talk him into staying or make accommodations in order to keep him. She also knew he needed to be all in or he wasn't the best person for her and her children. Both were right in their honest assessment of the situation, and it led to the hard decision: It was time to go their separate ways.

Don't agree to marry without both of you having a clear commitment that you can trust.

A Reasonable Expectation That Your Kids Are Open to a New Family and Will Be Blessed by It

Let me define some terms in this statement. It's not reasonable to think your kids are open to having a stepparent and stepfamily if you have talked to them about it only a couple of times, if you have had a rapid first-date-to-engagement timeline, and/or if you think their fears are silly and assume they'll get over them after the wedding. These aren't reasonable expectations; they're fantasy. You also can't be sure without some objective input.

One of the best things a single parent can do is to invite an extended family member, a youth pastor, family friend, or grandparent to spend time listening to the children talk about their feelings related to the potential stepparent, his or her children, and the possibility of becoming a blended family. Kids just aren't as transparent with their biological parent as they are with someone objective that they trust. In chapters in both *The Smart Stepmom* and *The Smart Stepdad* on later-life blended families, I share, for example, stories about adult children who told their widowed parent how excited they were that their parent was considering remarriage—only to later reject the stepparent after the marriage was final. Was the adult child lying? No. They, like younger children, have mixed feelings all at once and can genuinely be happy for their parent and sad for themselves at the same time. Inviting a trusted mentor or family member to explore both sides of the child's feelings will give you objective feedback that can help you decide whether to move forward and what is the best timing. As I said in chapter 5, your children do not get to decide whether you marry. But only a fool doesn't care whether they like the idea or hate it.

The second part of the section heading should go without saying, but I'm going to say it anyway. Don't marry someone unless you are convinced they will bring emotional, spiritual, psychological, and relational blessings to your children. This is your first obligation in making a decision to marry (not your personal happiness). God has entrusted your children to you, so

When the Kids Are Adults

A common mistake is assuming that adult children will have few adjustments to a parent's remarriage. Be sure to talk with them extensively and explore how life will change for everyone if a wedding takes place (see chapter 10).

you must consider the stewardship of their lives a vital priority in making a decision for marriage.

"YEAH, BUT HOW DO I *KNOW*?"

Now, having said all that, let me really frustrate you by stating the obvious. Even if your confidence in both couple and child relationships is high, mutual commitment is present, and a willingness to give the best of yourself in the loving service of the other is being lived out, you still won't *know* that you should get married. At some level when you get right down to it, marriage is a leap of faith. There are no guarantees.

Recently I had dinner with a couple about to be married; their wedding date was about a month away. Megan had two children from a previous marriage that ended in divorce. Ryan, her fiancé, had never been married and didn't have any children. One source of stress for the couple was Megan's ex-husband, who was unpredictable and irresponsible, and a consistent fly in their ointment. But there was a lot of positive energy around Megan's young kids, who loved Ryan and couldn't wait for the couple to marry so he could "spend the night."

As we talked, I began to pick up on Ryan's apprehensions. As much as he loved Megan and her kids and wanted to join his life to theirs, he found himself wondering if he could follow through with the decision to marry her. The crux of the matter centered on what Ryan couldn't control. As a single man, Ryan had been the master of his universe. A man who loved being in charge of his schedule, things, and family relationships, Ryan was now being challenged by circumstances and people (e.g., Megan's ex-husband) that he could not predict, let alone control. He feared walking into something that would be a constant thorn in his manageability flesh. Did he want to marry Megan and her children? Yes. Did he *know* that doing so would work out well? No.

No one can *know*.

I told Ryan two things. First, he didn't have to get married. Even though an announcement had been declared, plans had been made, and a date was set, he didn't have to get married. He could bow out gracefully or just slow down the love train until his confidence increased.

Second, I attempted to calm his anxiety around not knowing. Wanting to be certain that things would work out was, ironically enough, a reflection of his need to control his life. If he married, he would have to do so knowing that he would never be certain about anything and certainly not in control of his world (something singles without kids often miss). Rather, he would have to trust God to teach him and Megan who they needed to be and trust that his and her commitment to each other would provide a protective climate around their relationship that would allow them to learn what God had to show them.

What Ryan—and you—can never know before marriage is who he needs to become in order to love his spouse and family. God will teach him that, and he'll use the crisis of marriage, parenting, and life to show him what that looks like. For Ryan to put his faith in some constructed reality of what he knows is extremely nearsighted. At the end of the day, he will be much better off putting his faith in God's ability to show him how to love, even while God is also showing Megan how to love.

What I'm saying is this: *Even after dating well (and you ought to), exploring your fit as a couple, examining your fears (and you must), listening to and considering your kids' needs, and pausing at every flashing yellow light (and you should), marriage is still a leap of faith.* And it's in the falling that God teaches you to love another person the way his Son loves you.

The decision then is this: Are you willing to leap and take your kids with you?

GAINING CONFIDENCE

Confidence calms the heart and reduces anxiety. If some concerns are keeping your confidence low, I would encourage you to pursue resolution of those issues. But even if your confidence is high, it can be based on unrealistic expectations and assumptions—a figment of your imagination. For example, some have a blind confidence in their future, assuming that stressors during dating will automatically improve after a wedding. "Once we're married and have more time together, we'll be able to work through these things," I heard one woman say. WRONG! Problems that exist before marriage tend to worsen after.

So how do you know if you have a false confidence? How do you resolve issues so you can consider the future? Get objective feedback. Here are two things to do.

Email question: "I'm aware that both of us are weak in managing money. Should we hold off on marriage until each of us improves in that area, or is it okay to remarry, since we're both aware of the weaknesses?"

Reply: "Confidence should be coupled with skills. Hoping a problem will magically go away is asking for trouble. Grow in your money management skills before becoming engaged."

Pre-engagement Counseling

I know you've heard of premarital counseling, but when your confidence about marriage is faltering, I suggest you seek out pre-engagement counseling. Sitting down with someone can really help you stay objective about the relationship and avoid being blinded by the fog of love. Explore your concerns and frustrations with someone, both individually and as a couple. This will help you make a more informed decision about marriage and perhaps work through some issues that may be lowering your confidence.

Take the Couple Checkup

You may have taken the Checkup earlier in your dating relationship, but feel free to take it again now. If gains have been made, you'll see it in black and white. If not, you'll see that, too. Either way, you're getting valid objective feedback on the overall health of your relationship.

"WE'RE ENGAGED!" MAKING ANNOUNCEMENTS AND TELLING THE KIDS

Because confidence is high, each of you trusts the other's resolve, and the kids are on board, you've gotten engaged. Congratulations! It's time to make it known to the world.

I'm going to make an assumption (which is always danger-ous, by the way!). If you get engaged, it will not be a surprise to your kids. If they are blindsided by it, you've probably skipped a step (go back and read chapter 5). Assuming you've been having an ongoing dialogue about your relationship and their feelings about it, and assuming your dating has moved at a pace that has allowed them to see its growth and have time to bond with your partner (and if present, their children and extended family), then the engagement announcement should not be a huge surprise to them. It will certainly be a reality check—but it should not blindside them. Still, you have to tell them.

Telling the Kids

Given the diversity of children's ages, genders, personalities, developmental needs, and family history (e.g., family closeness, parenting history, loss events, etc.), it would be absurd for me to tell you exactly how you should tell the children about your engage-ment. Instead, I'll share some things for you to consider and the two of you can pray for wisdom as you decide how to proceed. In addition, when I asked my focus group of single parents what worked for them, a number of best practices rose to the surface. Let's learn from two case studies.

Kelsey shared, "Before we got engaged, we had already been preparing the kids for many months, telling them we were moving toward marriage. In the beginning we sensed some resistance, but as they came to see the difference in us as a couple, they have come to accept the situation." Let's notice a few things that are important. First, not only had Kelsey and her boyfriend been defining their relationship to each other, they had been defining it to their children, as well. When the time for engagement came, it wasn't a surprise because the kids had a few months to prepare themselves emotionally and express any concern.

Second, by having multiple conversations with the children over time, this couple strengthened their leadership voice with the children. Including them invites respect from children even while the kids' input helps the adults to objectively evaluate the possible fit of family members. The couple will also be wise to continue having multiple conversations throughout the engagement period about life after the wedding, changes the children will have to face, and how they feel about all that is happening (see chapter 10). Ongoing dialogue is crucial to staying emotionally connected and helping the family journey forward.

Third, note that the reality of marriage initially brought some child resistance to the surface—it usually does. We'll talk more about that later in this chapter.

Another single parent, Melissa, and her fiancé, Bruce, reported this when asked how they told their kids about their engagement. "We have kept open lines of communication with both our children throughout our dating. Before he proposed, he sat down with his kids and I sat down with mine and we talked openly about what they thought of the other partner. Also, because my kids' father passed away, Bruce and I wanted to make sure they understood that he wasn't replacing their dad, but was just going to be a father figure. We asked my kids if they thought their dad would approve of Bruce helping me to raise them; they said yes."

I love that Melissa and Bruce spoke individually to their children. If the other partner and their children are in the room when you tell them you're engaged, you might not get a completely honest response. Better to create an environment conducive to freedom of expression. Next, note that right from the start they proactively defined for the kids some of the implications and boundaries of the new family. By telling them that Bruce wasn't going to replace their father, they helped the kids know what to expect from him and what they didn't have to fear in him. Another helpful strategy is to provide as many facts as possible about how their lives will change after the wedding. For example, share "Here is our timeline for a wedding and where we will live; this is where you'll go to school; and here's what we're going to do to ensure that your time with your mom/dad in the other home is maintained."

Melissa and Bruce also showed honor to the kids' deceased biological father and kept his place in the family alive by asking what he would think about Bruce stepping into their lives. This declares that their approach of forming the blended family will be one that expands the emotional system of the former family and includes family members past and present, rather than one that tries to shrink the emotional system and cut out important people. At a time when so much is changing, children need to hear this from their parent and future stepparent and then see this spirit of grace lived out day after day.

Tips for Telling the Kids

- Emphasize your commitment and availability to them.
- Plan for and engage in multiple conversations before and after the big announcement.
- Acknowledge that this means change for their lives in significant ways; try to anticipate some of those changes.
- Provide as many facts as you can about how life will change, and give honor to their other family loyalties and relationships.
- Don't let your enthusiasm cheat them of time with the other household.
- Don't be surprised by volcanic eruptions.

Melissa made one more comment. She noted that she and Bruce have daughters the same age that competed often. When planning how to make their announcement, they tried to anticipate the issues they would have and tried to be sensitive to their needs by individually reassuring each that she was loved. I would extend this strategy to every child (not just those in competition with a future stepsibling). Bathe your pre-, during-, and post-announcement conversations in reassurance of your love and commitment to them. One of the predictable reactions from children to a parent's engagement announcement, especially those who have already lost connection with a parent or significant family member, is a feeling of insecurity. Life is about to change—*again*—in another huge way. Kids need to know they haven't lost your love, attention, nurturing, or availability. Reaffirm your love for them over and over.

Volcanic Eruptions. From time to time, even after couples have done due diligence in preparing their kids for an engagement and feel confident the children are in favor of the marriage, children erupt when an announcement is made. Others erupt after the wedding. This unforeseen eruption can be explained this way: It isn't real until it's real. Only when the realities hit home do some children experience resistance and anger at the idea of their parent's marriage (not unlike the sinking feeling most of us get as our wedding day approaches and the "Dear God, what have I done?" question hits our brain).

When this happens, the trick is not to panic. What is needed is a turning toward the child's negative emotions and the courage to coach them into understanding what they are feeling and what they will do with it. A couple who responds negatively to a child's reaction will likely do one of two things: either dismiss their feelings (defensively try to explain to the child why they don't need to feel that way), or back away from the engagement decision to placate the child. Neither is helpful. Instead, recognize that the eruption is a function of fear and insecurity and articulates how significant this change is for the child. Refer back to the discussion of Learn to Tune In and Turn Toward in chapter 8, and acknowledge the child's feelings so you can earn the right to coach them through the negative emotions and insecurity. This is not to say that you can resolve the child's fears; this is not about fixing them. It is about remaining connected to them and their pain.

Telling Parents, Extended Family, and the Children's Other Parent

Talk with your fiancé and perhaps the children (if they need a voice in how this happens) and decide how to inform your extended family and your ex-spouse about the engagement. They, too, have a vested interest in your life and the lives of the children and will need to be respectfully considered. A principle to keep in mind when deciding who should tell whom is that blood talks to blood and ex-spouses talk to ex-spouses. Each of the adults should tell their own extended family members and ideally the children's other biological parent. An exception to the latter would be if doing so will erupt violence or a hostile response from an ex.

PLANNING OR PREPARING?

Once everyone knows about your engagement, it's time to start preparing. Unfortunately, once engaged, most people shift gears from working on a relationship to planning a wedding. But engagement is just the beginning, a passing from a phase of evaluation to a new phase of preparation, that is, preparing to become a family. In the next chapter I'll outline some key steps to take and what to look for as blended family living approaches.

Discussion Questions

1. To what degree do you agree with this statement and why? I think it's getting harder in our culture today for people to pull the trigger on a covenant commitment to another person. The collective anxiety in our world about the instability of marriage screams, "Don't do it!"

2. In what way does the Christian culture scream, "Go ahead, get married—everything will be fine!"

3. This chapter outlines four basic points to assess before becoming engaged:

   - confidence in your relationship
   - conviction that you are willing to give your life away in the loving service of the other (and their children)
   - trust that your partner is willing to do the same for you
   - an educated, objective sense that the children are reasonably open to your union and a new family, and that their emotional, psychological, and spiritual health will be well served by your marriage.

   What do you think of them? Would you add more?

4. Now rate your current relationship on each point above on a scale of 1 to 10 (10 being the highest). Explain your rating.

5. Share what would be difficult about being in a relationship where one is ready to marry and the other isn't.

6. Discuss this statement: *Even after dating well (and you ought to), exploring your fit as a couple, examining your fears (and you must), listening to and considering your kids' needs, and pausing at every flashing yellow light (and you should), marriage is still a leap of faith. And it's in the falling that God teaches you to love another person the way his Son loves you.*

7. Review and discuss these tips for telling the kids once a decision to marry has been made. What additional ideas would you add to the list?

- Emphasize your commitment and availability to them.

- Plan for and engage in multiple conversations before and after the big announcement.

- Acknowledge that this means change for their lives in significant ways; try to anticipate some of those changes.

- Provide as many facts as you can about how life will change, and give honor to their other family loyalties and relationships.

- Don't let your enthusiasm cheat them of time with the other household.

- Don't be surprised by volcanic eruptions.

Chapter 10

Preparing for a Good Blend

If remarriage, as Samuel Johnson said, is the triumph of hope over experience,[1] then a harmonious blended family is the triumph of risk over fear, trust over self-protection, inclusion over exclusion, and grace over possessiveness.

Congratulations! The decision to marry has been made, perhaps a date set, and you're planning a wedding. Just be sure to plan for becoming a family, as well, because ultimately that is what this is all about—becoming family to one another. Through the years I have encountered countless blended families that were comprised of a strong marital couple who really loved each other trying to exist within a divided stepfamily household. Preparing for a good blend will hopefully keep that story from becoming yours.

BECOMING FAMILY: KEY STEPS TO TAKE

Don't be surprised if you feel underprepared for stepfamily living. In the national survey of couples planning to form blended family marriages, which David Olson and I conducted, we found that in two-thirds of unhappy couples (those with struggling couple relationships) one or both partners felt inadequately prepared for the realities of stepfamily living; so did one-third of the happy couples. We also found that 78 percent of couples were already having difficulty related to blending and 72 percent disagreed about whether getting married would put more stress on their relationship (this disagreement, ironically, puts more stress on their couple relationship).[2] The point: Don't be surprised by growing stress and tension around how to blend. It's not easy even in all-around healthy situations.

> As the wedding day approaches, stress tends to increase for all family members. Don't be surprised by this.

I often tell pastors that the key objective of stepfamily ministry is to get the newly formed family through the first few years. Surviving the "integration years" is really what you're trying to do. On the surface that may not sound like much, but actually it's rather significant. The first five to seven years are when everyone is adjusting to life together and becoming family, that is, learning first to like each other and then, perhaps, to love each other even as they are psychologically redefining their existing family to include new family members. This is a stressful process with many potholes and road hazards. For example, research confirms that "it takes longer for children to adjust to living in a stepfamily than it does for them to adjust to living in a single-parent family."[3] That statement usually hits single parents right between the eyes, because they remember how much stress and strain their children experienced after the death of their parent or the divorce in their family. I believe the adjustment time will be reduced by a healthy dating process (what this book has outlined) but the point is, expect there to be a period of transitional stress for your home after the wedding.

Further, while most adults intuitively know that stepparents and stepchildren can take years to bond, most biological parents don't anticipate that relationships with their own children can come under stress, especially within the first two years after the wedding and again when young children enter adolescence. Mother-daughter relationships post remarriage, for example, commonly become strained (even as mother-son relationships often get better when a stepfather enters the home), and the family unit as a whole can experience three times the level of stress that a biological family experiences. The good news, however, is that this escalation of stress and conflict generally recovers after two years.[4] Again, the issue is adjustment to the new family.

Some may ask, "Ron, are you trying to scare us? Why include these doses of reality at this point in the book?" No, I'm not trying to scare you, but I am trying to inform you that while good dating requires much work, more work will be needed after the wedding. Don't relax your initiative; move instead into this next season of your relationship with as much drive as you've had up to now because, while the integration years may be stressful for many (not all) blended families, the rewards are worth the price. Research confirms that once the marriage and blended family stabilizes, parenting improves, relationships with children improve, and child outcomes improve.[6]

> "Remarriage does not constitute a neutral event for children. Parent-child relationships are put under considerable stress following remarriage, and parents and children face challenges that are not experienced by parents in first-marriage and single-parent families."[5]

I'm convinced that healthy stepfamilies are a redemptive work of God for both children and adults, but that's a function of years of dedication, determination, and smart stepfamily living, not just good dating.

This chapter cannot present a comprehensive overview of smart stepfamilies (read *The Smart Stepfamily: Seven Steps to a Healthy Family* to get that), but I can share a few core concepts to get you started.

Solidify Your Marriage: Parent as a United Front

In the digital era, it's rare to receive a snail mail letter. One day I opened my mail and received this heartfelt petition addressed to me but, I think, written to *you*.

> *Dear Ron,*
>
> *I don't know why I'm writing this letter to you.*
>
> *Unfortunately, four and a half years into a second marriage, I realize that I've always been in the #2 position behind my stepsons in my wife's heart. I've heard and read how serious this is but did not fully understand until experience caught up with me. Now, with my stepsons determining how my wife interacts with them and with me (and my children alienated from me), I now see what a grave mistake I made.*
>
> *Please continue to tell spouses that God designed marriage for them to be #1 in each other's hearts, and that straying from this design will never, ever work. Of course, I'm not referring to a spouse who is abusive or following one who is contrary to Christ. I'm referring to the majority of spouses in stepfamilies who are doing their best but find themselves in second place, with their spouse deferring to and trusting the children rather than them.*
>
> *I'm three to six months away from divorce at this point. . . . I have always been #2 and after years of spiritual work and determined effort I've not been able to move to #1.*
>
> > *Respectfully,*
> >
> > *Joe*

Unfortunately, Joe encountered the Achilles' heel of blended family integration—a biological parent who is unwilling to boldly move their spouse into a place of prominence in their heart and family. You simply will not bond or grow together in love if this dynamic is true in your marriage.

Joe referred to being #1 or #2. Talking about rank sometimes frightens biological parents because they think this means abandoning or neglecting their children. It unequivocally does not! This isn't about leaving anyone behind, but it is about prioritizing the marriage as a lifelong commitment and positioning the marriage as the parenting team and focal point for leadership in the home. Couples in first marriages raising their biological children do this, as well. Yes, they devote a great deal of time and energy to raising and nurturing their children, but the kids also know that Mom and Dad don't hide things from each other, are deeply loyal to each other, and are a united team in leading the home. This understanding empowers the couple and provides stable leadership within the home. Of course, in a biological family kids are as equally invested in their parents' marriage as the couple is; that is, they want Mom and Dad to be loving and committed to each other. In a newly formed blended family, however, some children are threatened by the marriage and feel pushed aside by it. That means the first time Mom says, "I know I used to give you quick answers, but now I need to ask my husband what he thinks before making a decision," they may challenge Mom's effort to position the stepfather as a co-leader. And the first time she takes her husband's side on an issue, they may hit the roof.

But she must do just that. If she does not, she tears the family's Achilles' heel.

However, if she does express and live out her commitment to her husband, she positions him and herself to parent from within the marriage. They must be a unified team or everything begins to crumble.

> **What Kids Are Feeling**
>
> One reason kids sometimes react strongly to changes within the family is the feeling that they are being forgotten or pushed aside. Of course, they are not being neglected, but after experiencing much loss in their lives, it can feel that way to kids. Have compassion for how difficult this is for them, but gently persist in uniting as a parenting team.

Because parenting in stepfamilies is extremely different than in biological families, I have written two books on the subject (*The Smart Stepmom* and *The Smart Stepdad*). Let me summarize the process this way: Attachment—the emotional and psychological bond that affords a parent the right to lead—is automatic for the biological parent but must be developed over time with the stepparent. Until that bond exists, stepparenting is a very tenuous experience with fragile boundaries, tightrope circumstances, and explosive scenarios. The biological parent must keep the role of disciplinarian in the life of the child (hopefully they played this role during the single-parent years) while the stepparent slowly joins the parenting process and earns the right to lead.

On occasion, young children will bond quickly and fast-forward through the typical two to three years that stepparents need to accomplish this, but with most children, patience is critical. Not expecting instant love and being patient with affection in the stepparent-stepchild relationship is also important to the stepparent's evolving role. Anything that demands a place in the child's heart rather than letting it happen on its own usually backfires on everybody. That's why you cook a stepfamily in a Crockpot, not a blender.

Cooking With a Crockpot

Just because you're engaged (or newly married) doesn't mean you can accelerate your rocket to Passion Planet at light speed with the expectation that your children will also accelerate theirs (see chapter 5). That would be trying to combine your stepfamily in a blender—quickly and with high velocity. It is far wiser to adopt a Crockpot cooking style—slowly with low heat.

In *The Smart Stepfamily* I wrote, "Stepfamilies need *time* to adjust to new living conditions, new parenting styles, rules, and responsibilities. They need *time* to experience one another and develop trust, commitment, and a shared history. They need *time* to find a sense of belonging and an identity as a family unit. None of these things can be rushed. People who are trying to prove to their parents, friends, church, minister, or *themselves* that their remarriage decision was right for everyone, need their family to 'blend' quickly. But they are often greatly disappointed and feel like failures. A slow-cooking mentality . . . invites you to relax in the moment and enjoy the small steps your stepfamily is making toward integration, rather than pressuring family members to move ahead."[7]

The great paradox of adopting this approach to integrating your family ingredients is that it helps everyone relax about being family. No heavy pressure (which just invites resistance from kids). No upside-down "you need to take care of me by loving the people I've inserted into your life" burdensome messages from adults. No "forget your past, end your loyalties, and get happy now" crazy talk. Just calm "we respect your confusion and accept you anyway" patience and mature leadership. This, over time, paradoxically fosters openness and connection—just what you're looking for.

Here are some contrasts to help you adopt a Crockpot strategy to family integration:

- A blender mentality assumes that because children are happy that you're getting married, they won't ever also feel confused and sad by it. A Crockpot mentality expects some "hitting the brakes" reactions from the children at some point (weddings commonly bring this on).

- A blender mentality forces children to call a stepfather "Daddy," but a Crockpot mentality lets them decide on their own.

- A blender mentality expects everyone to be happy with the new family, but a Crockpot one finds calm when there's tension, knowing that they're not done "cooking" yet.

- A blender mentality expects that combining all holiday and other special-day traditions will make everyone pleased, but a Crockpot mentality says "try it and see," knowing that it may take a few years to figure out what actually works.

- A blender mentality makes children take down pictures of loved ones, but a Crockpot one encourages honoring deceased family members and staying connected with extended family.

Cooking Time

Younger "ingredients"—under the age of five—may require far less time to soften toward stepparents than those between the ages of ten and fifteen years. Also, on occasion a stubborn ingredient may resist softening and retain a sour taste. In either case, keep cooking and don't unplug the Crockpot!

- A blender mentality assumes adult children will "be mature about this," but a Crockpot one gives them space to be hurt.

- A blender mentality declares, "I do so much for them—I should get more respect than this," but a Crockpot one says, "I give freely to my stepchildren and trust that with time they'll show gratitude."

- A blender mentality says, "My kids should not have to be disappointed, so my new spouse will just have to deal with my catering to their pain," but a Crockpot mentality says, "I can be loving to my kids and still allow them disappointment—besides, catering just keeps them stuck in their pain and doesn't invite them to grow through it."

If any of the above challenged your thinking or left a pit in your stomach, you're catching on. Merging two families into one is not as simple as toasting bread. It's more like discovering by trial and error a recipe for a casserole of ingredients you've never combined before. Getting smart about the process will help a great deal, but even then there are some things you'll just have to discover with God's help all on your own. Trust him to show you how.

CROCKPOT EXERCISES AND RECOMMENDATIONS

To aid your healthy cooking process, I suggest you involve the ingredients of your future family in these exercises. As with the ongoing dialogue with your children about dating, these activities are meant to be assessment and intervention. They will give you information and insight into your children and family dynamics, and hopefully move you forward as you prepare to be a family.

They are not listed in any particular order; feel free to apply those that make most sense to your situation and revisit the themes as needed. Younger children may not need all of these, but pre-teens, teenagers, and adult children will likely benefit from all of them.

How Shall I Introduce You? Exercise

Background: The terms we use to refer to one another indicate how we define a relationship and the level of closeness we feel, and give respect to the role the relationship plays in each person's life. Children use labels to indicate the emotional attachment they feel with someone. A stepparent who started off being referred to as "Sara, my dad's wife" may become "Mom" in a few years, but not if the biological mother is within hearing distance. The stepmom who adapts to changing labels shows respect for a child's close tie with their mother and welcomes their own growing connection with the stepchild.

Purpose: To engage future family members in a proactive discussion of their current and future relationships. You hope to decide together what terms you will use, and in the process communicate respect for one another.

Process: Both adults should arrange a time to sit down with the children. If you both have children, have two meetings to encourage openness. The biological parent should take the lead and say, "The reason we wanted to talk with you today is to discuss how we will introduce one another once we get married. I realize this can be complicated and a bit awkward at times, so let's figure it out together. Before we start, we [indicate you're speaking for the couple] want you to know that we don't expect you to use any particular term when referring to us. You are free to use whatever label makes you comfortable as long as it also feels respectful to us. Plus, we also know that you have a lot to worry about when choosing labels. Things like whose feelings might get hurt or what others will think. Feel free to be honest with us about this stuff. Also, we know each of you may have different preferences—that's okay. Just speak for yourself." Then engage these questions:

- Once we are married, in public how would you like to be introduced by your stepparent? In general should they say, "This is my stepson/daughter," or "my wife's son/daughter" or something else? What feels okay and what's weird about this?

- In private (in our home), what term would you like for them to use when talking to you or about you (e.g., "buddy" or "my son/daughter")?

- [The stepparent can ask] In public, how would you like to introduce me? When talking about me, what term feels most fitting?

- In private, what would you like to call me?

- What would you like to call your stepsiblings? Stepgrandparents? Other family members?

- Now that we've decided this, when do you think these terms might be awkward (e.g., if your other parent is present)? What term would you like to fall back on at that point?

- We suspect that for all of us, these decisions will need to change at some point. Don't hesitate to let us know if you want to make a change, or just go ahead and change it and we can discuss it later.

Special Tips: The point of this exercise is to help family members not fret over what others think or how they interpret certain terms. Anything you can do to put them at ease is wonderful. Also, if a child uses a term of endearment sooner than you are prepared for, don't ask them to stop unless you have a significant fear of them doing so, and then the biological parent should be the one to ask the child not to. If a child wants to call a stepmother Mom, let them. I know it's respectful toward the biological mother to reserve that term only for the mother, but the child can feel rejected by the refusal. Most kids are good at measuring their loyalties and comfort zones. Trust them to do so. For more on this matter, read "The Name Game" at www.smartstepfamilies.com/view/name-game.

What Will Change? Exercise

Background: Because a parent's marriage brings loss to a child, helping them anticipate and be prepared for those changes shifts what they can't control toward what they can. By the way, before having these discussions with the children, you will need to discuss them as a couple and have in mind what you consider optimal before you talk to the children.

Purpose: This exercise readies kids for coming adjustments, communicates that you are aware of how marriage complicates their lives, and reveals your consideration of the other household and their extended family relationships.

Process: The couple should arrange a time to sit with each set of children and explore how things will change after the wedding. Be as practical as you can and explore as many topics relevant to their lives as you can. The examples below are just a brief list of possible topics. Once you have this formal conversation, you'll be able to have additional spontaneous conversations as you think of more topic areas.

Start by saying something like, "You know, we got to thinking about all the things that will change once we get married. Some of them are going to be welcome changes, others will be beyond your control. Let's try to think of as many as we can and talk about them."

- What's one thing you are really looking forward to? I'll go first . . .
- What's one thing you aren't looking forward to? Again, I'll go first . . .
- Home: Discuss changes in bedrooms, bathroom use, kitchen use, TV/computer/media time, etc.
- Church: Will you stay at your current church or find a new one? How will you decide?
- Routines: How will your morning routine change? Daytime? Nighttime? Weekend?
- Traditions/Holidays/Special Days: How will you celebrate birthdays and special days? What traditions will you keep and which ones will have to be modified? How will holiday schedules/traditions change? (Don't try to negotiate every tradition, just discuss a few examples and note that you'll have to figure out the specifics of each as they come up.)
- Expectations and Chores: If both of you have children, by now the kids have already sized up the differences. What general expectations/rules will be the same, which will change? What chores will children be responsible for? Explain what the kids should expect if they misbehave and who they will hear from.
- Boundaries: With stepsiblings in the house together, does there need to be a dress code? Under what conditions can you enter someone's bedroom? If you have a problem, who do you talk to?
- Money: How will allowance and discretionary money matters with the children change? Who pays what bills, and what responsibilities do the children have for lunches at school, jobs, etc.?

- Time Together/Activities: More people in the family means less time with parents. Anticipate for the kids what this might mean for them and reassure them of the things that you are committed to continuing (e.g., a special nighttime ritual with a child). Acknowledge that it will be more difficult to keep certain rituals of connection, and grieve this reality (e.g., going to lunch regularly with an adult child).

- School: Will they have to change schools? If so, where and when? What are the pros and cons of this?

- Social Life: Will they be able to see their friends as much? If so, how? What avenues do they have for staying in touch?

- Visitation and Extended Family Relationships: It is vital that your marriage not interfere with the kids' visitation schedule; they need continued, predictable contact with the other household, and your blended family should not cost them that. Even while reassuring them of this, discuss what might change in terms of logistics. (For example, "We will live closer to your dad's house, so it will take less time to get there—that's a good thing!")

Special Tips: Reading through this list and considering the implications for your children ought to cause you to pause and reflect on all that will be required of them. Remember that change, especially if you didn't ask for it, equals loss and powerlessness (for kids and adults alike). Don't be surprised if this conversation isn't a little depressing for them. Be prepared to be compassionate.

Recognized Loss Exercise

Background: As has been pointed out, remarriage is a gain for the adults and initially a loss for the children because it brings unwanted changes. But this isn't the first loss for the children. This is loss added on top of an already existing loss story. Furthermore, loss reminds us of previous loss and erupts again the grief associated with it. For example, a parent's remarriage can resurrect a child's sadness over their parent's death. Compassionately meeting a child in the midst of their loss helps them journey through it.

Purpose: Recognizing that becoming a family carries some loss is important to maintaining emotional influence with the child. To be distant and removed from this part of the child's life is to appear uncaring and disengaged. Rather, strive to show yourself a trustworthy asset to the child as they cope with what life continues to throw at them.

Process: Try to engage the child in a dialogue about loss. Lead with your own experience of grief and then acknowledge theirs.

- If you were widowed: "I got to thinking about something the other day. As excited as I am to marry Jane/John, it makes me miss your mother/father. I miss the way she/he would . . . Has my engagement made you miss them, too?"
- If you were divorced: "I know our divorce has put you through a lot and I grieve what cannot be for you. I was thinking, if I were you, I'd be a little sad that . . . (e.g., you're going to have to get used to a stepmom/dad/stepsiblings in the house). Or maybe you're feeling hurt or angry that I'm getting married because . . . (e.g., this means your mother/father and I can't get back together). Or maybe you are worried how this will impact your mom/dad. Is any of that on your mind?
- What's hard for you to get used to as you think about our marriage and new family?

Special Tips: Remember to emotionally coach your child through the loss conversation and acknowledge their sadness, don't dismiss it (see chapter 5). This isn't about fixing the pain, it's about joining them in it and hugging their hurt.

Wedding Planning Activity

Background: Weddings mark the start of a new journey for every member of the blended family. While the making of a covenant during the wedding is very significant for couples, it does not necessarily bind children to a stepparent. However, including them in the planning of the wedding and the wedding itself can have a bonding impact.

Purpose: Including children in wedding planning gives them an opportunity to voice their desired level of involvement. Including a family medallion ceremony within the wedding affirms biological children of their parent's continued commitment to them and serves as a bonding experience for the whole family.

Process: Engage the children in planning the wedding as appropriate to their age. Listen to their ideas and respect their desired level of involvement.

Also, consider presenting a family medallion to the children during the wedding. Just as a wedding ring signifies covenant love between a couple, a family medallion communicates the intended desire of the parents to become family to and for one another.

Special Tips:

- Learn more about the family wedding service and the use of a family medallion here: www.smartstepfamilies.com/view/family-medallion.
- Links to remarriage bridal showcases and blended family wedding planners can be found here: www.smartstepfamilies.com/links.php.
- A recommended resource for anticipating and planning the complexities of a blended family wedding is *Weddings, A Family Affair: The New Etiquette for Second Marriages and Couples with Divorced Parents, Second Edition* by Marjorie Engel (Carpentaria, CA: Wilshire Publications, 1998).

Pre-Stepfamily Counseling

Background: While the average cost of a wedding is $27,500, less than a third of first-marriage couples seek premarital preparation, and less than 25 percent of pre-stepfamily couples do. That is stunning to me, especially when you take into account that premarital counseling works. Premarital preparation can reduce the risk of divorce by 30 percent,[8] and a meta-analysis of eleven experimental studies found significant differences favoring couples who received premarital education, with a 79 percent improvement in all marital outcomes compared to couples who did not receive premarital education.[9] Reading this book is a solid start, but it's nothing like getting you and the kids in counseling. That's right—I said the kids should be part of the process, too.

Purpose: The personal attention a counselor can give you and the children is invaluable. The objective feedback and insight will serve you well as you step into the future and give children a neutral place to talk through their concerns or fears.

Process: Find a qualified pastor or stepfamily therapist who has had training in understanding blended families (for tips, see this article: www.smartstepfamilies.com/view/findtherapist). Likely you will experience a combination of individual, couple, and entire family sessions that can identify potholes and remove stumbling blocks.

Special Tips: Unfortunately, finding a pastor or counselor with blended family training is difficult. If you can't find someone with training and experience, share Smart Stepfamily resources with a premarital counselor and invite them to do some extra homework for you. Start by giving them this web link: www.smartstepfamilies .com/view/counselor.

Get Connected: Attend a Local Blended Family Small Group or Class

Background: Being connected with a fellowship of faith is vital to our spiritual growth. Being connected to a class or small group of stepfamily couples is also vital to your family's growth.

Purpose: Attending as a premarital couple will not only get you connected, but help you find insight and support from others a little further down the road than you.

Process: Get involved with the blended family ministry at your church. If they don't currently have one, ask them if you can start one; I have written guidelines and resources to help you get started (smartstepfamilies.com/view/educate). If necessary, attend the blended family ministry of another church in your area. After getting to know the couples in the group, ask one of the couples to be your mentors. Specifically, ask them if they will meet with you monthly until your wedding and then for the first two years of your marriage. Explain that you don't expect them to have all the answers; they would just act as a sounding board for you.

Keep Reading As a Couple

This chapter is far from comprehensive in addressing the total integration of your stepfamily—there's a whole series of books for that. To really get prepared, before and after the wedding, may I suggest you pick up a copy of my other books *The Smart Stepfamily, The Smart Stepdad, The Smart Stepmom* (coauthored by Laura Petherbridge), and *The Remarriage Checkup* (coauthored by David H. Olson). Each will make a unique contribution to your family preparation.

A FINAL ENCOURAGEMENT

You're about to marry the wrong person.

That doesn't sound very encouraging, does it? Well, it really is. What it means is this: If you were perfect, you could pick and marry the right person. But since you're not, you'll pick the wrong person—who, of course, in God's economy is the right person. That is, the right person to help God reveal what you didn't know about your selfishness or frailties or limitations and to grow you beyond them. Furthermore, God will use the journey of marriage and becoming a blended family to sharpen you, refine you, and teach you how to love with humility, sacrifice, and surrender, just as Christ has loved you. That is, God will do all these things if you will let him.

I suggest you do.

A toast to your new family: *May God's richest blessings be upon you, and may grace rule in your home.*

Discussion Questions

1. Learning that the average stepfamily needs five to seven years to settle into their new family identity and roles can be both encouraging and discouraging. What is your reaction?

2. Becoming family is in part about psychologically redefining your existing family to include new members. How might that be stressful for children in your situation? For adults?

3. Why do you think it's tempting for couples headed into marriage to relax their initiative, that is, stop working on "becoming family"?

4. React to this statement: The Achilles' heel of blended family integration is a biological parent who is unwilling to boldly move their spouse into a place of prominence in their heart and family.

5. Why do you think positioning the stepparent as part of the parenting team is the biological parent's responsibility?

6. React to and discuss this statement: Attachment, the emotional and psychological bond that affords a parent the right to lead, is automatic for the biological parent but must be developed over time with the stepparent. Until that bond exists, stepparenting is a very tenuous experience with fragile boundaries, tightrope circumstances, and explosive scenarios. The biological parent must keep the role of disciplinarian in the life of the child while the stepparent slowly joins the parenting process and earns the right to lead.

7. Review the contrasting statements between a blender mentality and a Crockpot mentality in chapter 10. Discuss each one individually, but also discuss what the cumulative "blender" or "Crockpot" impact would be on the family as a whole.

8. Review each of the Crockpot Exercises and Recommendations in chapter 10. Discuss which ones you will implement and why.

- How Shall I Introduce You?
- What Will Change?
- Recognized Loss
- Wedding Planning Activity
- Pre-Stepfamily Counseling
- Get Connected: Attend a Local Blended Family Group or Class
- Keep Reading

9. Looking back over the entire book, what concept stands out as most helpful to you in your circumstances? What have you remembered most?

APPENDIX 1

SOCIAL NETWORKING DO'S AND DON'TS FOR SINGLE PARENTS

HELEN WHEELER, LPC

- After divorce, filter out pictures and friends that now create vulnerability for you and the kids.
- Broadcasting your co-parenting frustrations makes you vulnerable and hurts your children. Keep in mind that malicious ex-spouses can track your involvements and use the information against you. Assume everything you write can end up in court.
- Be wary of reigniting old flames (e.g., high school). You aren't that person anymore and neither are they.
- Moderate your need for social connection with an awareness of the costs of social networking (your kids are watching). Remember, once you hit Send, you can't get it back or control where it ends up.
- Monitor your children's involvement on sites and set time boundaries on use. Take advantage of cell phone and website parental control options.

SAMPLE PURITY PLEDGE

Managing sexual temptation is tough for every person. Talking through your standards and deciding together to seek purity can help. Review this sample purity pledge and decide which parts you can agree to and abide by. The pledge is adapted from the Marriage Ministry, Watermark Community Church, Dallas, TX, Marriage Team, 2012.

• • •

We believe that sex is a gift from God to be enjoyed in the context of marriage, and that he had our best in mind when he gave us strong directives about sexual purity before marriage. There are many benefits to staying sexually pure before marriage. By waiting until marriage:

- you please God
- you will be able to develop a much clearer conviction of how God is working in your relationship
- you build the trust that is necessary for true intimacy and for lifetime commitment
- you develop the godly qualities of patience and self-control
- you affirm that you care more for the other person than yourself

- you protect yourself from feelings of guilt and shame
- you provide yourself with an example to give your children and others
- you help protect yourself from the emotional, mental, and even physical trauma that can come when you break off a relationship
- you have a greater opportunity to develop a stronger emotional and spiritual bond—you can develop healthy communication habits and skills, and discover more about each other than just the physical
- you prevent unwanted pregnancy
- you increase the anticipation and enjoyment of your wedding night
- you experience the blessing of obedience
- you discover more about each other than just the physical
- as a Christian, you maintain a witness to the world
- as a Christian, you avoid bringing reproach on the name of Christ[1]

Although many couples believe engaging in sex prior to marriage will strengthen their relationship, we believe the opposite is true. We believe sex outside of marriage can slow down the growth of a couple's relationship by causing emotional confusion and distracting couples from pursuing activities that would be more meaningful and beneficial during the dating/engagement stage of a relationship. We believe it is worth noting that research indicates a positive relationship between couples who live by biblical standards regarding purity and marriage longevity.[2]

While physical intimacy is of huge importance in a healthy marriage, we do not believe it is the *foundation* upon which to build a great marriage. Therefore, the aim of this pledge is to help each couple focus on the essential building blocks of establishing a healthy marriage.

What is outlined below is a voluntary pledge—taken by a seriously dating or engaged couple—to sexual purity. This pledge is optional but **strongly** encouraged. Therefore, we ask you to consider agreeing to limit your physical involvement, as indicated below, and be held accountable by your mentor couple.

Sexual purity means much more than not having sexual intercourse before marriage. Many couples avoid intercourse but are still sexually intimate. Scripture defines sexual purity as being morally excellent. And moral excellence means being holy. It means avoiding the appearance of evil. It means purity of thought as well as purity of deed. It means protecting one another's innocence from being stained by impure actions.

Those considering or preparing for marriage are asked by their mentors to talk about the pledge privately and pray about it before deciding whether to take this step. Regardless of what the decision is, the matter will remain a private one between the marriage mentors and you. Ultimately, however, it is a spiritual matter between you and God.

Be honest about the physical part of your relationship. We know the Bible does not specifically address how far a couple can go before marriage. However, it is clear that we are to flee from sexual immorality (1 Corinthians 6:18). Consider making a commitment to keeping your physical activities between items 1 and 4.

1. Holding hands
2. Hugging
3. Light kissing
4. French kissing
5. Kissing on the neck, ears, or other parts of the body
6. Indirect stimulation of the breasts/genitals (i.e., "grinding")
7. Manual stimulation of the breasts/genitals

8. Oral stimulation of the breasts/genitals

9. Intercourse/anal sex

If your physical activities exceed #4, we suggest the following steps:

- Confess your sin to the Lord and repent of your actions (Psalm 51:3–4).
- Confess and seek forgiveness from your partner.
- Inform your mentor couple. The man must contact the male mentor within twenty-four hours after exceeding the physical limit. If the man does not do so, the woman will call the female mentor.
- Calling your mentor does not circumvent the need to confess your actions to God; however, letting your mentor know keeps you accountable so your focus can be on the spiritual, character-building issues that are important in forging a lifelong committed marriage.

We pledge to hold our relationship to a biblical standard so the Lord might bless this relationship now and in the many years ahead. Therefore, we agree to call our mentors if the physical involvement goes beyond level 4.

PREMARITAL COUPLE   MENTOR COUPLE

....

....

• • •

Selected Scripture related to sexual purity:

Flee from sexual immorality. Every other sin a person commits is outside the body, but the sexually immoral person sins against his own body.

—1 Corinthians 6:18 ESV

But sexual immorality and all impurity or covetousness must not even be named among you, as is proper among saints.

—Ephesians 5:3 ESV

For this is the will of God, your sanctification: that you abstain from sexual immorality; that each one of you know how to control his own body in holiness and honor, not in the passion of lust like the Gentiles who do not know God; that no one transgress and wrong his brother in this matter, because the Lord is an avenger in all these things, as we told you beforehand and solemnly warned you. For God has not called us for impurity, but in holiness. Therefore whoever disregards this, disregards not man but God, who gives his Holy Spirit to you.

—1 Thessalonians 4:3–8 ESV

Let marriage be held in honor among all, and let the marriage bed be undefiled, for God will judge the sexually immoral and adulterous.

—Hebrews 13:4 ESV

NOTES

Introduction: Striving for Love

1. Justin Rocket Silverman, "Something Old, Something New: After 30 year courtship, a bride keeps a promise on groom's 100th birthday," *The Daily,* Monday, May 2, 2011, www.thedaily.com/page/2011/05/02/050211-news-old-folks-1-3/.

2. Belinda Luscombe, "Who Needs Marriage? A Changing Institution," *Time,* November 18, 2010, www.time.com/time/magazine/article/0,9171,2032116-2,00.html.

3. Christians definitely believe in marriage—even after divorce. One study found that conservative and mainline Protestants are more likely to remarry after divorce than those with no religious affiliation. And the more important religion is to a person and the more they attend worship, the more likely they were to remarry (S. M. Brown, "Religion and Remarriage Among American Women: Evidence From the National Survey of Family Growth," (master's thesis, Mississippi State University, 2007), http://www.open thesis.org/documents/Religion-remarriage-among-american-women-384370.html

4. I'm grateful to author and speaker Laura Petherbridge for this insight. Personal communication, October 21, 2011.

Chapter 1: Dating in a Crowd: Dating With Purpose

1. David Popenoe and Barbara Dafoe Whitehead, "The State of Our Unions 2001: The Social Health of Marriage in America," report published by Rutgers, The State University of New Jersey, June 2001, www.virginia.edu/marriageproject/pdfs/SOOU2001.pdf.

2. Michael Lawrence, "Stop Test Driving Your Girlfriend," Boundless.org, April 8, 2010, www.boundless.org/2005/articles/a0001306.cfm.

3. Scott Croft, "Biblical Dating: An Introduction," *Boundless webzine*, November 2006, www.boundless.org/2005/articles/a0001401.cfm.

4. Previously unpublished data from the National Survey of Couples Creating Stepfamilies project by David H. Olson and Ron L. Deal.

5. E. M. Hetherington and J. Kelly, *For Better or For Worse: Divorce Reconsidered* (New York: W. W. Norton & Company, 2002), 197.

Chapter 2: Mirror, Mirror on the Wall: Am I Ready to Date?

1. See Webster's Dictionary: www.merriam-webster.com/dictionary/recover.

2. See 1 Corinthians 7:10–11. Paul urges couples not to divorce, but if they do, to reconcile or remain unmarried. Also, in Matthew 19 when asked by the Pharisees if

Jesus subscribed to an "any cause" divorce, Jesus' first response clearly communicates that he was not interested in validating the reasons people give to divorce, he was only interested in upholding God's original intent that husband and wife remain one. In other words, husbands and wives remaining together in a God-honoring, mutually loving relationship is valued by God.

3. Please note that many abusive partners will use spiritual guilt to try to manipulate a spouse into coming back, blaming the victim for leaving the marriage when, in reality, it was the abusive partner who "left" the marriage by breaking their vows to love, honor, and cherish long before the divorce.

4. Trusted author Laura Petherbridge includes a discussion of forgiveness and reconciliation in her book *When "I Do" Becomes "I Don't": Practical Steps for Healing During Separation & Divorce* (Colorado Springs: David C. Cook, 2008).

5. **The Bible on Divorce and Remarriage.** I believe that Christians should strive to rightly handle the Bible and receive it as the infallible Word of God for our lives. I also believe that we can trust God to look out for our best interests (even when Scripture is confronting our choices and behavior). Therefore, understanding God's will for divorced people as it relates to remarriage is to gain wisdom for how to live. I wish I could easily summarize for you what the Bible teaches about divorce and remarriage. I can't. I'm just not that smart. There have been a number of scholarly works done on the subject of marriage, divorce, and remarriage in Scripture. They are quite extensive and interesting to read (and I suggest you read at least a couple). But here's the problem: The scholars don't agree. Read three books and you're likely to end up with three different conclusions about what Scripture teaches, not to mention the implications for your situation. Talk to three pastors and again, you'll likely end up with three different opinions, at least on certain details. It really is a confusing topic of study.

So instead of sharing my understanding of Scripture on this matter let me make the most practical suggestion I can. Part of being a Christian is walking through life with a group of Christians; we call it church. I hope you're a part of one, because it is there that we encourage, support, and hold each other accountable as we live as Christ-followers. And it is there that you can gain understanding from the pastoral team as to their expectations for how you manage your spiritual responsibilities as a divorced person. You need to do your own study of divorce and remarriage in Scripture, but you also need to walk out your choices in community with others and under the guidance of your local church. If you are part of a local church, you have submitted yourself to their leadership and should seriously consider their teaching about divorce and remarriage. I realize different churches teach different things, but our call as Christians is not to shop for the church that tells us what we want to hear, but to receive the wise counsel of Scripture. If your understanding does not match that of your pastor, don't immediately reject his, but do continue to seek guidance from other spiritual leaders as you search out God's heart for your circumstances.

Chapter 3: Ready or Not, Here I Come: The Readiness Factors

1. Ron L. Deal, *The Smart Stepfamily: Sevens Steps to a Healthy Family* (Bloomington, MN: Bethany House, 2006), 25–30.

2. D. L. Blackwell, "Family structure and children's health in the United States: Findings from the National Health Interview Survey," *Vital Health Stat* 10 (2001–2007): 2010.

Chapter 4: The Fear Factor: Preparing Yourself and the Kids for Dating

1. Leigh Baker, *Protecting Your Children From Sexual Predators* (New York: St. Martin's Press, 2002), 16.

Chapter 5: Kid Fears and Dating Considerations

1. Judith Wallerstein and Sandra Blakeslee, *What About the Kids? Raising Your Children Before, During, and After Divorce* (New York: Hyperion, 2003), 280–282.

Chapter 6: Finding Love in All the Right Places . . . and in All the Right Ways

1. Helen Fisher, "The Brain: How We Fall in Love, and How We Stay Together," *Family Therapy Magazine*, May/June, 2011, 23.

2. How Honest Are You on Social Networking Sites? Poll results reported in *USA Today*, Friday, September 30, 2011.

Chapter 7: Yellow Light. Red Light. Green Light.

1. S. Browning, "Why Didn't Our Two Years of Dating Make the Remarriage Easier?" *Stepfamilies* (Summer 2000), 6.

2. Learn the signs of an abuser at www.smartstepfamilies.com/view/abuser.

3. Daniel Wile, *After the Honeymoon* (Oakland, CA: Wile Publications, 1988), 12.

4. John M. Gottman, *The Science of Trust: Emotional Attunement for Couples* (New York: W.W. Norton, 2011), 25.

5. Edwin H. Friedman, *A Failure of Nerve: Leadership in the Age of the Quick Fix* (New York: Seabury Books, 2007), 211.

6. W. Bradford Wilcox, PhD, "Why Marriage Matters: An Argument for the Goods of Marriage," online video, August 16, 2011, www.centerforpublicconversation .org/events/v/wmm-20110816.php (accessed 8-26-11).

7. David Olson and Amy Olson-Sigg, "Overview of Cohabitation Research: For Use with PREPARE-CC," (Minneapolis: Life Innovations, Inc., 2005).

8. M. M. Sweeney, "Remarriage and Stepfamilies: Strategic Sites for Family Scholarship in the 21st Century," *Journal of Marriage and Family* 72 (2010): 667–684.

9. A. J. Cherlin, *The Marriage-go-Round: The State of Marriage and the Family in America Today* (New York: Alfred A. Knopf, 2009), 18–24.

10. S. M. Stanley, G. K. Rhoades, and F. D. Fincham, "Understanding romantic relationships among emerging adults: The significant roles of cohabitation and ambiguity" in F. D. Fincham and M. Cui (eds.) *Romantic Relationships in Emerging Adulthood* (Cambridge, England: Cambridge University Press, 2010), 234–251.

11. L. Waite and M. Gallagher, *The Case for Marriage: Why Married People Are Happier, Healthier, and Better Off Financially* (New York: Doubleday, 2000).

12. Ibid.

13. Ibid.

14. Ibid.

15. Stanley, Rhoades, and Fincham.

16. Ibid.

17. D. Popenoe and B. Whitehead, "Should we live together? What young adults need to know about cohabitation before marriage," The National Marriage Project, New Brunswick, NJ, 1999.

18. Ibid.

19. This finding by Dr. Scott Stanley is highly significant because it makes women, in particular, vulnerable to men who aren't fully committed to the relationship. Men need to make a clear decision for marriage, not slide into it and later feel unsure of their commitment. See Stanley, S. M., Rhoades, G. K., & Markman, H. J. (2006). Sliding vs. deciding: Inertia and the premarital cohabitation effect. *Family Relations, 55*, 499–509.

20. Stanley, Rhoades, and Fincham.

Chapter 8: Going Deeper

1. Timothy Keller with Kathy Keller, *The Meaning of Marriage: Facing the Complexities of Commitment with the Wisdom of God* (New York: Dutton, 2011), 192.

2. Gottman, 176–201.

3. Ibid., 193.

4. Marjorie Smith, "Resident Mothers in Stepfamilies" in *The International Handbook of Stepfamilies: Policy and Practice in Legal, Research, and Clinical Environment,* Jan Pryor (ed.), (Hoboken, NJ: John Wiley and Sons, Inc., 2008), 163.

Chapter 9: Re-Engage? Decisions About Marriage

1. Gottman, 174–175.

Chapter 10: Preparing for a Good Blend

1. Samuel Johnson, quote referenced February 2012, www.samueljohnson .com/marriage.html#89.

2. Ron L. Deal and David H. Olson, PhD, *The Remarriage Checkup: Tools to Help Your Marriage Last a Lifetime* (Minneapolis, MN: Bethany House, 2010).

3. Claire Cartwright, "Resident Parent-Child Relationships in Stepfamilies," in Jan Pryor (ed.), *The International Handbook of Stepfamilies: Policy and Practice in Legal, Research, and Clinical Environments* (Hoboken, NJ: John Wiley & Sons, Inc, 2008), 215.

4. Ibid., 212.

5. Ibid., 213.

6. Ibid., 215–216.

7. Deal, *The Smart Stepfamily*, 69–70.

8. S. M. Stanley, P. R. Amato, C. A. Johnson, and H. J. Markman, "Premarital education, marital quality, and marital stability: Findings from a large, random household survey," *Journal of Family Psychology* 20, no. 1 (2006): 117–126.

9. J. S. Carroll and W. J. Doherty, "Evaluating the effectiveness of premarital prevention programs: A meta-analytic review of outcome research," *Family Relations* 52, (2003): 105–118.

Appendix 2: Sample Purity Pledge

1. Adapted from *Preparing for Marriage: Discover God's Plan for a Lifetime of Love* by David Boehi, Brent Nelson, Jeff Schulte, and Lloyd Shadrach (Ventura, CA: Gospel Light Publications, 2010), 99.

2. Joan Kahn and Kathryn London, "Premarital Sex and the Risk of Divorce," *Journal of Marriage and Family* 53 (1991): 845–855.

Ron L. Deal is husband to Nan (since 1986) and proud father of Braden, Connor, and Brennan. Everything else is just details.

Ron is a marriage and family author, speaker, and therapist. He is founder and president of Smart Stepfamilies and director of Blended Family Ministries for FamilyLife. Ron is author of *The Smart Stepfamily*, *The Smart Stepdad*, and *Dating and the Single Parent*, and coauthor with Laura Petherbridge of *The Smart Stepmom* and with David H. Olson of *The Smart Stepfamily Marriage*.

Ron is a licensed marriage and family therapist and licensed professional counselor, who frequently appears in the national media, including *FamilyLife Today*, *Focus on the Family*, *HomeWord*, and *The 700 Club*. He is a popular conference speaker, and his video series *The Smart Stepfamily DVD* is used in communities, churches, and homes throughout the world. Ron is a member of Stepfamily Expert Council for the National Stepfamily Resource Center and is a featured expert on the video curriculum *Single and Parenting*. Ron and his wife, Nan, and their sons live in Little Rock, Arkansas.

For more about Ron and his ministry, visit *RonDeal.org* and *SmartStepfamilies.com*